Does Someone at Work Treat You Badly?

Does Someone At Work Treat You BADLY?

LEONARD FELDER, PH.D.

BERKLEY BOOKS, NEW YORK

A notice from the author and the publisher:

The ideas, procedures, and suggestions contained in this book are not intended as a substitute for consulting with a physician or an attorney. All matters regarding your health require proper medical supervision and all matters regarding your legal rights require proper legal guidance.

Anyone who has a history of psychiatric disorder, who feels emotionally unstable, or who is taking major tranquilizers or antidepressant medication should not do the exercises in this book without first consulting a qualified mental health professional.

DOES SOMEONE AT WORK TREAT YOU BADLY?

A Berkley Book / published by arrangement with
the author

PRINTING HISTORY
Berkley mass market edition / June 1993
Berkley trade paperback edition / July 1999

The Penguin Putnam Inc. World Wide Web site address is
http://www.penguinputnam.com

ISBN: 0-425-16512-4

BERKLEY®
Berkley Books are published by
The Berkley Publishing Group, a division of Penguin Putnam Inc.,
375 Hudson Street, New York, New York 10014.
BERKLEY and the "B" design are trademarks
belonging to Penguin Putnam Inc.

PRINTED IN THE UNITED STATES OF AMERICA

10   9   8   7   6   5   4   3   2

Acknowledgments

There are far too many people to thank individually for their insights and assistance with this book. There have been hundreds of therapy clients, workshop participants, friends, and colleagues who have contributed valuable gems to the case studies and ideas contained in these chapters.

To thank just a few who helped a lot, I want to state my appreciation to Lucky Altman, Teri Bernstein, Patricia Birch, Harold Bloomfield, Catherine Coulson, Glen Effertz, Ted Falcon, Frank and Kathy Fochetta, George Gamez, Melinda Garcia, Joan Graff, Crystal Jones, Arlene Levin, Alice March, Laura Pawlowski, Helene Pine, Marie Poll, Peter Reiss, Lew Richfield, Cheryl Sindell, Marc Sirinsky, Lorna Siroko, Janet Sternfeld, Neil Van Steenbergen, Sirah Vettese, and Linda Waddington.

In addition, I want to express my heartfelt gratitude to my clinical supervisor, Dr. Janet Ruckert, for her excellent guidance.

Two other crucial people who believed in this project and offered important feedback and assistance are my agent, Connie Clausen, and my editor, Elizabeth Beier.

I also want to thank my family members for their love and insights, especially Martin and Ena Felder, June and William Schorin, Janice and Craig Ruff, Edward Rothenberg, Jeffrey Schorin, and Ruth Wilstein.

Most of all, I appreciate the wisdom, creativity, and love my wife, Linda Schorin, has given me on this and my other books. I am very lucky to have a partner who understands and contributes as much as she does.

*This book is dedicated to
those men and women who confided in me
about their frustrations at work and
who had the courage to do something
positive to improve their situation.*

The names and occupations of each of these individuals have been changed to protect confidentiality.

Contents

Does Someone at Work Treat You Badly?

1

Who's Giving You Aggravation at Work?

Do you have days when the frustration at work truly gets to you? Are there days when you sense it's time to do something about it?

An intelligent and creative woman named Marta arrived late one Thursday evening to the weekly support group I've been running for the past few years. She looked tired.

Marta told the group on that Thursday night she felt a lot worse than just tired. She was exhausted, hadn't been sleeping well, and was thinking about quitting her job.

For several weeks, Marta had been keeping us informed about her struggles with Gordon, a man at work who she had described as condescending, manipulative, dishonest, extremely controlling, and very short-tempered. Sounds like a real sweetheart of a guy, doesn't he? The kind of person we all look forward to seeing every day at work!

Marta was exhausted not only because she was battling constantly with this extremely difficult individual. She was upset because, as she described:

I feel trapped. I wish I could quit this job and find a place where the people are more sane to work with.

1

I've been asking around, looking at the classifieds, making a lot of phone calls, and I've gone on a few interviews. But I've learned that right now is not a good time for people in my line of work. Some call it a recession, some call it a sluggish recovery. I call it being trapped having to work with a monster. I'm exhausted from the stress of dealing with his constant abuse and right now I have to hang in there no matter how unpleasant it gets.

Does Marta's frustration from working with a difficult person sound familiar to you? Is there someone in your daily life—a difficult boss, coworker, customer, supplier, colleague, or business partner—who treats you badly? Have you thought about quitting but decided this isn't the right time? Have you tried to improve the situation with this aggravating individual, but you've been unsuccessful in making any progress?

A Breakthrough

I've discovered in my research and counseling that there are a huge number of women and men who face the daily frustration of having to deal with an extremely unpleasant or abusive individual at work. As in Marta's case, no matter how hardworking, intelligent, or creative you are in your job, you might still be the target of someone who is a terror to work with.

However, on this particular Thursday night, there was a breakthrough for Marta. After weeks of attending the support group sessions and looking closely at her frustrating work situation, Marta had made three important discoveries:

1.   Gordon was not going to change his difficult behavior unless Marta first changed the way she related to him.
2.   In order to change the way she responded to Gordon

and other difficult people at work, Marta was going to need some specific techniques for becoming emotionally stronger and more professional, even when Gordon treated her badly.

3. In order to remain strong and professional in high-pressure situations, Marta was going to need to keep doing certain journal writing exercises, visualization exercises, and role-playing exercises that we have practiced in group sessions.

Using these and several other exercises that are described in this book, something shifted for Marta that Thursday night. She began to feel and act much stronger. Two weeks later, she arrived with a smile on her face and told the rest of the group, "I did it! I absolutely, positively did it!"

"Did you quit your job and find another one?" someone in the group asked.

"No," Marta said. "Much better than that."

"What happened?"

Marta explained:

I had an important meeting this morning with Gordon and for the first time in months I felt like he treated me with some actual respect. I used some of the techniques we had discussed in group. I had done a lot of internal work and some journal writing the past few weeks to make sure I was in good shape for dealing with Gordon and not becoming intimidated by him again. I also changed the way I looked at Gordon and the way I talked to him. Instead of feeling and acting like a cautious victim, I felt and acted like a quality professional.

I knew ahead of time what I could say to him that might make him defensive and controlling, and what I could say to him that would get him to respond favorably and cooperate with what I needed from him.

I'd done my homework like we discussed in group, but I was still pretty amazed that he actually listened to what I was saying and he treated me like an intelligent professional. I never thought it could happen—to see obstinate, obnoxious Gordon treating me like a respected colleague. I loved it.

Despite Marta's initial triumph with Gordon that week, I have to interject at this point that this was not the end of her struggles with him. It took three more months and several additional techniques before Marta became even more professional and respected in her dealings with Gordon.

Like many of my clients who sought counseling after being victimized by a difficult individual at work, Marta had successfully transformed her situation into a personal and professional triumph. She told the group members on the night several months later when she finally left the support group,

I used to feel helpless and frustrated at work when someone like Gordon treated me in a demeaning fashion. Now I've got options and ways of responding. Now I've got the inner strength to handle things better no matter how challenging the person might be.

A Revealing Look at Your Own Work Situation

Like Marta, many hardworking men and women face the challenge of dealing with an extremely unpleasant individual at their jobs. Let's examine your own situation closely for a moment. Just how much are the tensions at your job affecting you? What side effects are created by friction between you and the person (or persons) who have been treating you badly? Exactly how big a price are you paying by allowing this situation to continue to weigh on your mind?

Here's a test you can take to find out if your work

situation is affecting your own personal and emotional health. Simply answer each question, and be honest with yourself.

1. In the past few weeks or months, have you had difficulties with anyone at work—a boss, coworker, colleague, employee, customer, supplier, or business partner?   ____ Yes   ____ No

2. Do you sometimes dread having to see this person at work or in social situations, or have you ever felt anxious when he or she has called and left a message for you to return the call?
    ____ Yes   ____ No

3. Have you begun to have conversations in your head with this person, or arguments in your mind where you defend yourself or try to explain your side of the conflict?   ____ Yes   ____ No

4. Have you ever been inundated with thoughts about this difficult individual when you are trying to fall asleep, or when you wake up in the middle of the night, or when you are trying to relax on a weekend or a vacation?   ____ Yes   ____ No

5. Do you find yourself second-guessing your own performance or feeling self-critical as a result of your interactions with this unpleasant individual?
    ____ Yes   ____ No

6. Is your creativity blocked or is your clarity of mind hampered somewhat by the lingering discomfort of having to deal so often with such a difficult person?
    ____ Yes   ____ No

7. Have you noticed that you have been trying to calm yourself down after work lately by eating more, drinking more, or smoking more than is healthy for you?   ____ Yes   ____ No

8. Are you becoming more impatient or short-tempered at work due to your tensions with this person?   ____ Yes   ____ No

9. Have you become more susceptible lately to colds,

flus, stomach problems, or muscle aches in your neck, shoulders, or back? Is it possible that you are carrying a lot of physical tension in your body as a result of the emotional tension you are feeling toward this individual?   ____ Yes ____ No

10.   Do you sometimes feel resentful that this individual treats other people at work a lot better than she or he treats you?   ____ Yes ____ No

11.   Do you find yourself wondering why you are sometimes singled out for criticism or harsh treatment while at the same time you haven't been acknowledged by this individual for the things you've done well?   ____ Yes ____ No

12.   Have you begun to dislike your job or have you thought about quitting as a result of this unpleasant situation with a difficult individual?
____ Yes ____ No

13.   Have you noticed that you are more irritable or impatient with your spouse or lover, or with your children or your friends as a result of your leftover frustrations from your situation at work?
____ Yes ____ No

14.   Is your paycheck or your financial security being jeopardized by the unresolved tensions between you and this person?   ____ Yes ____ No

15.   Have you let some projects go sour or lost some good opportunities for advancement because you are unable to overcome the obstacles put up by this unpleasant individual?   ____ Yes ____ No

16.   Are you feeling discouraged that this person has continued to treat you badly despite your efforts to improve the situation?   ____ Yes ____ No

Scoring

Add up the number of times you answered yes to the questions listed above. Then see which of the following groups you fall into.

- If you said yes to none of the above questions, either you have a terrific work situation, or else you have been unemployed for quite a while.
- If you said yes one to five times in the above questions, you have identified the first signs that the tension at work might be starting to affect your physical and emotional health. If the problem continues, the side effects may worsen.

  Your challenge is to make sure you do something constructive to improve the situation before the problem gets worse. If you wait until you or the other person are completely fed up with the situation, it becomes much harder to make progress. So don't wait until you are at your breaking point before taking some of the action steps described in the following pages.
- If you said yes to six or more of the previous questions, then there definitely is a serious problem at work. Don't let anyone tell you to just ignore it or let anyone convince you that it goes with the territory. This problem at work is causing you enough emotional and physical distress to warrant serious attention. Most importantly, the problem is not going to simply disappear with the passage of time. The longer you continue to feel powerless or victimized in this situation, the more these side effects will continue to worsen.

You are not alone in having a difficult situation at work. Nearly everyone at some time or other has at least one difficult individual at work who at that moment seems like an unsolvable problem. But in most cases there are several useful things you can do to improve the situation. Don't feel ashamed or discouraged for being in a tough situation with an unpleasant individual, but remember that the sooner you face up to the problem, the sooner you can do something positive about it.

Exactly What Kinds of Difficult People Are You Facing?

Taking the right steps to deal with an aggravating individual at your job begins with understanding exactly what kind of person you are facing. I have found that the vast majority of difficult people at work can be described as one of six different types. How many of the following types, which will be covered in more detail later in this book, sound like someone you've worked with?

The Angry Screamer

Like a time bomb ticking away in the middle of a stressful work situation, the Angry Screamer is often on the edge of exploding. How do you stay strong and professional when an intimidating boss, coworker, customer, or supplier is screaming at you? How do you make sure you don't keep getting victimized by this kind of person? What can you do to teach this person to direct his or her anger toward something else instead of dumping it on you?

The Saccharine Snake

How do you recognize when you are dealing with someone whose smile is a bit too saccharine, or whose ''Have a nice day'' conceals an extremely manipulative or competitive personality? Will you know when this person is about to steal your shorts or do something else that you need to stop? How do you protect yourself without stooping to this person's level?

The Space Case

Have you ever worked with someone who has that faraway look in his or her eyes as though nobody is awake in there, who is showing up at work but leaving his or her brains at home? Have you encountered someone in your job who is so spacey, inept, forgetful, apathetic, or distracted that he or she is a source of constant frustration? Learn how to be more successful with a Space Case and not fall into the traps that infuriate most people who try to deal with this kind of individual. How to bring out the competent side of a Space Case will be discussed with specific examples.

The Invalidator

Have you ever worked with someone whose mission in life is to find fault and pick at everything? How to spot an Invalidator, how to handle this kind of person, and how to deal with your own Inner Critic will be explained. Instead of feeling victimized by the overly critical person you work with, you will have tools and options for improving this potentially dreadful situation.

The Cold Shoulder

How do you deal with someone who is hard to reach, hard to pin down on a decision, or suddenly unavailable because of some wall he or she has put up toward you? If someone at work is giving you the Cold Shoulder, it can feel terrible, especially if this person used to be a reliable friend or colleague that you could turn to during a crisis. Learn what to do if someone is trying to exclude you, ignore you, or keep you in the dark. This book offers examples of people who successfully warmed up even the coldest shoulders at work.

The Testosteroni

There are certain men, and a few extremely aggressive women as well, whose sexual advances are hellish to deal with in the workplace. If you have been sexually harassed at work, what are your options? If you have been treated badly because of your gender, what can you do about it and still feel safe showing up at work? Sexist game playing and harassment in the 1990s is usually a lot more subtle and covert than it was in previous decades. How to recognize a

Testosteroni, how to take the right steps to protect yourself, and how to choose an appropriate response will be explored.

Why I Am Optimistic That Your Situation Can Be Improved

For the past fifteen years, I have been collecting stories about what really goes on in the workplace. I've been fascinated by the descriptions told to me by intelligent and competent men and women who nevertheless were mistreated at work. These were women and men like you and me, who deserve to be treated with respect at work but who unfortunately have come up against extremely difficult coworkers, business partners, customers, bosses, and others.

For the past fifteen years I've also been developing exercises and techniques for dealing with abusive or unpleasant individuals at work. I am optimistic about how these techniques can help your own work situation. They consist of:

- Creative ways to take care of yourself when you're forced to work with someone who is potentially hazardous to your emotional health
- Effective ways to stand up for yourself and your ideas without overreacting, getting fired, alienating people, or being mistreated even worse
- Successful ways to change the treatment you receive from certain difficult individuals. Even if these individuals don't change their abrasive style in general, you will be able to change the specific way they deal with you.

These techniques and exercises were developed from a variety of experiences in my own career.

In my first several jobs during and after college, I learned firsthand what it's like to work in high-pressure situations with some extremely unpleasant individuals. Thank goodness for the obnoxious people I met in those jobs; without them, I would never have been motivated to collect the material that has led to this book.

As a graduate student at the School of Management of the University of Pittsburgh in the 1970s, I asked my business and psychology professors to assist me in uncovering all the existing research and theories on why there is so much nastiness in the workplace and what can be done about it. What causes people to be so vicious or dishonest at work? Are there ways to deal with difficult individuals and not get victimized by them?

Later, as the manager of the research department at Doubleday and Company in New York, I spent a great deal of time learning from colleagues and coworkers specific tips on how they stayed sane and healthy in a cutthroat business like publishing, which in the 1970s began to change from a pleasant industry into a vicious battle of competing conglomerates.

Still later, I worked as the manager of strategic planning for American Express in New York, where I consulted with dozens of men and women who had become skillful experts on how to survive in the highly stressful world of financial services. After learning all I could about office politics and survival at American Express, I ''left home without it.'' I moved to California to complete my Ph.D. in psychology.

As a therapist and consultant for the past ten years, I have been testing out various approaches for helping decent men and women respond more effectively to some of the more vicious and insensitive people they encounter at their jobs.

Finally, for the past five years I have been leading seminars on winning at office politics for women and men from a variety of professions. At each seminar I am still fascinated by the stories people tell about how they were mistreated at work by bosses from hell, customers on the edge of insanity, employees whose minds are out to lunch, and business partners who have the morals of a cockroach.

From these experiences, I have discovered in my own

work life how to make sure I don't get victimized by individuals who are looking for someone to mistreat or manipulate. I've also counseled hundreds of women and men on how to make sure they don't get victimized by anyone at work who is difficult.

There are no guarantees, but my experience tells me that if you put into practice the insights and strategies contained in this book, you will see some improvements in your work situation.

These improvements are possible, even if the other person doesn't change all that much. You will be shown how to make sure this difficult individual treats you differently, even if he or she continues to be an unpleasant or troublesome individual in general. In other words, you don't need to change this person's basic personality in order to get him or her to change the way he or she deals with you specifically. All you need to learn is how to respond more effectively when this person does something that frustrates you at work, and how to teach this person that you are not an easy target for his or her future attacks.

Getting treated better at work is something that can make a tremendous difference in how you feel about your job and how you feel about your life. I urge you not only to read the suggestions and techniques in this book, but also to put them into practice in your daily work situations. If you follow the instructions, you will gain a variety of crucial skills and effective responses. The only thing you have to lose is your painful sense of victimization.

2

Exactly What Happened?

If someone tells me in a therapy session or at a seminar that they're frustrated or mistreated at work, one of the first things I do is to take a history of exactly what's been happening. What's been causing the pain or frustration? What's been making this person dread having to work with a certain individual?

Take a few minutes right now to jot down in a notebook your own observations, recollections, and feelings about the situation at work that has been getting on your nerves.

This written exercise can serve you in a number of ways.

1. It gives you a chance to sort out exactly what happened that made you feel mistreated at work. Who said what? Who did what to whom? When did the mistreatment begin? How long has it been going on? Who was a witness to any of the incidents? Who has been told about what's been taking place? Who understands your point of view? Who is supportive of your position, and who is not?
2. It allows you to put your memories and recollections in writing while they are still fresh and clear. Instead

13

of carrying these details and feelings around forever inside your head, you can lighten your load a bit by putting them down in a notebook for safekeeping.

3. Your written account of what's been going on at work can also become an important piece of evidence if you ever need to defend yourself in a wrongful termination case, a worker's compensation case, or any other type of lawsuit. Even if you have no desire to pursue a legal case, this written documentation can also give you detailed reminders to help you recall important facts and details. By having this type of written chronological log of incidents in front of you, you will be better able to stand up for yourself in any upcoming meetings where the personality clashes are being discussed. If you ever need to fire someone or have someone fire a certain difficult individual, this written documentation of the most crucial incidents will be extremely helpful. Quite often the difference between being ignored or being taken seriously with regard to your struggles with an obnoxious person at work depends on the written evidence you have compiled.

4. From a psychological standpoint, there is something healing and empowering about putting your point of view in writing. It gives some credibility and substance to your private feelings. It helps you feel more professional and less victimized. It often can assist you in taking appropriate action and not remaining victimized. Keeping a written account of what's happening at work is the first step toward regaining your peace of mind and the possibility of feeling good again about your job.

What to Put in Writing

You can begin today keeping a complete list of incidents regarding this frustrating individual at work. Then make sure you continue to update this list whenever additional incidents occur.

Either once a day or once a week, take a few moments to compile a simple list of facts about the incidents that reveal the mistreatment you've been facing. In most cases, this list should be a private one. No one should see it except you. You can keep it at home in a safe place, or if you decide to bring it to work, make sure it is kept locked away or is unavailable to anyone but yourself. At some future date you may need to show it to other people, but in the meantime this list of incidents is your own source of clarity and empowerment.

On your list be sure to include:

1. The date and time of day for each incident.
2. The location and context for each upsetting event. Was it a public meeting? Who was in attendance? Was it a private conversation? Were there any witnesses? Was there a memo, a fax, a written summary of what was discussed, or any meeting minutes? Who was sent copies of those written descriptions?
3. If there is any written piece of evidence of what happened between you and this individual, be sure to save it.
4. If there is no written evidence, be sure to write down your immediate recollections of what was said and what happened. Just tell the truth as best you can and then put down the date and time of when you wrote down these facts.
5. Were there any previous agreements, promises, or policies that were violated by this individual? If possible, include any written items that show the promises or policies you were relying upon when this person broke his or her word. Are there any written contracts, memos, notes, faxes, phone logs, meeting minutes, answering machine tapes, or written recol-

lections that describe what was promised and how it differed from what transpired later?

6. Have you or anyone else spoken to this person to tell him or her to stop the behavior that you find objectionable or unprofessional? If there have been any warnings to this person, either orally or in writing, make sure you write down what was said, when it was said, and how it was received.

7. You might also write down any fears or concerns you have experienced as a result of what happened. In what way has this frustrating situation at work affected your health, your advancement, your financial security, your personal life, or your family or work relationships?

8. Finally, write down what in your opinion would be a successful resolution of the situation with this difficult person. What do you think would be best for the companies involved? What would be best for the individuals involved? If you were a consultant or a mediator called in to advise the various parties, what would you recommend to resolve the problem?

These eight items will form the basis for your documentation of what's been upsetting you at work. This is the first step to transform this situation from one of victimization to one of empowerment.

Here are some examples of how these written documentations have made the difference between winning and losing for some people. See if any of the following give you some ideas on how you might benefit from putting your feelings and observations into a written list of incidents.

Example #1: The Case of the Intimidated Agency Executives

Gillian is an intelligent and hardworking woman who got a new job ten months ago for a large nonprofit agency. Unfortunately, she is supervised by a woman named Harriet, who is highly volatile, frequently vindictive, and who goes out of her way to sabotage Gillian's professional contacts and projects.

When Gillian first tried to improve her working relationship with Harriet by taking her out to lunch and talking with her, it only made matters worse. Harriet seemed to try even harder to sabotage Gillian's work. When Gillian spoke with the director of personnel at the agency about the problem, she discovered that the personnel director and most of Harriet's professional colleagues were intimidated by Harriet and were unwilling to stand up to her.

Gillian was feeling victimized and powerless when she came to discuss these issues with me in counseling. However, over the next several months, Gillian not only worked on building up her emotional strength to be able to stand up to Harriet, but she also began to document in writing Harriet's broken promises, unprofessional actions, and petty behaviors.

With renewed inner strength and a long list of well-documented incidents and details about Harriet, Gillian called a meeting a few weeks ago with the director of personnel and two of the top executives of the agency. Gillian was nervous about whether these intimidated people would be willing to stand up to Harriet. During the meeting, the clarity of Gillian's arguments were reinforced by the extensive documentation she presented. The director of personnel and the two top agency executives were impressed by how thoroughly Gillian had documented what were clearly some unprofessional and harmful actions by Harriet.

Gillian recalls,

> At that meeting, the two top agency executives and the personnel director told me that for the first time they had enough written proof of Harriet's unprofessional behavior. People had complained verbally in the past, but no one had ever documented in writing exactly what Harriet does that is so clearly out of line.

As a result of Gillian's written documentation, the two agency executives and the personnel director realized that they no longer needed to remain intimidated by Harriet. They began discussing a three-month timetable to warn Harriet, observe if her unprofessional behavior changed at all, and eventually to fire her or transfer her to a less crucial department. They now knew that if Harriet sued them, they had enough written documentation to successfully defend themselves. If Harriet screamed at them, as she often did, they now felt there was enough professional support between the four of them who had attended the meeting to stand up for what each knew was best for the agency.

There is no guarantee that written documentation will get the same results in every situation or will convince your colleagues to overcome their fears and stand up to an abusive individual, but as this case demonstrates, I have found repeatedly in many difficult work situations that written documentation does make a difference. Even if people where you work have been putting up with someone's abuse for years without doing anything about it, something interesting and new tends to happen when you put your point of view in writing. It looks more official. It feels more solid. It no longer sounds like one person whining or complaining. The written documentation proves you are serious, professional, and worthy of being taken seriously.

Example #2: The Case of the Slippery Colleague Who Likes to Steal the Credit

Henry and Frank work together on several important research projects. Frank is willing to share the credit for their research ideas, but Henry has the habit of going to meetings with top executives and pretending the best ideas were his alone. Even if Frank contributed 70 percent of the thinking and hard work on a project, Henry repeatedly convinces top management that he deserves all the credit for the success of the project.

For almost two years, Frank has felt victimized by

Henry's stealing the credit on their projects, but Frank's sense of shyness and politeness prevented him from saying anything about it to Henry or anyone else. As Frank told me when he came for counseling,

> I'm a research professional with a huge load of projects to manage. I don't have time to get into petty arguments with Henry, and I'm not the kind of person who goes around tooting my own horn. But at the same time, I do resent being passed over for certain promotions, and I don't enjoy it when Henry gets a lot of praise and acknowledgment for things that he and I both know were my ideas.

Does this sound familiar to you? Have you ever worked with someone like Henry who had the frustrating habit of stealing the credit for things that were your ideas, or who refused to share the acknowledgment and rewards for what was clearly a collaborative effort?

Over a period of a few months in counseling, Frank and I discovered what was holding him back from standing up to Henry and getting the credit he deserved. First, we worked on Frank's fear of sounding conceited if he let others know of the hard work and good ideas he had contributed. Growing up with an angry, abusive father had made Frank extremely reticent about getting too much attention. He was afraid that if he spoke up on his own behalf, people might criticize him or ridicule him the way his father had done.

Second, we worked on Frank's fear of alienating Henry. According to Frank,

> Even though Henry is a pain in the ass, he's also a damn good researcher and a wealth of information on things that are helpful to our projects. I don't want to let him keep taking advantage of me, but I also don't want to confront him too aggressively and possibly lose him as a colleague.

Third, we began to make sure Frank put in writing not only the incidents for which he felt mistreated by Henry but also the positive things that both Frank and Henry contributed to each of their projects. I told Frank to keep the list of Henry's dishonesty private for now, but to send out a Confidential Weekly Progress Report to a select group of decision makers telling exactly what good ideas Frank, Henry, and others had contributed to their ongoing projects.

Frank began to put into writing and then send out in a weekly memo the specific ideas, steps, and hard work that were going into each research project. He made sure to spell out in writing what were his own ideas and contributions. Instead of giving Henry the chance to steal the credit at a later date, Frank was not only keeping top management informed about the progress of each of their research efforts, but more importantly, he was letting the top decision makers see in writing the specific accomplishments and good ideas that Frank had contributed.

In this Confidential Weekly Progress Report, Frank included what they were discussing, who had done what, and what was being accomplished on the various projects that were being researched. He also urged the decision makers who received the weekly memo to give him their suggestions on how to improve any of these crucial projects. Instead of being left out and excluded by Henry's boasting, Frank had regained control of the information flow. He now appeared to top management as the brains and vital center of the research activities. Simply by taking a few moments each week to put in writing what was going on, he had successfully prevented Henry from stealing credit from him any longer. In fact, after only a few weeks, these Confidential Weekly Progress Reports became so popular that many other decision makers were asking for copies. Frank and his supervisor had to limit the circulation of these crucial documents.

Because the credit-stealing issue had now been put in writing, Frank had solved the problem without a major confrontation or nasty battle with Henry. Frank's extensive documentation had made it clear to Henry that the collaboration was just as much Frank's good work as Henry's. As a result, Henry had to steal the credit only from less creative colleagues who didn't document exactly what happened during their collaboration on other projects with Henry. Henry could no longer pull his deceptions on any project that involved Frank and was written up in the weekly progress memo.

This case demonstrates how thorough documentation doesn't always have to lead to formal confrontations, firings, or legal cases. Sometimes merely by taking the step of writing things down and letting certain people know what's happening, you resolve a long-standing problem and you warn the difficult person to back off. Quite often the simple fact that the difficult person knows you have the truth all written out and formalized makes this person change the difficult behavior sufficiently to start treating you better.

This case also illustrates the fact that Henry didn't change his overall behavior. With other colleagues he still attempted to steal the credit whenever possible. But now Henry knew that because of the weekly written progress reports, Frank was no longer a pushover. Even if you can't change someone's basic personality or difficult behaviors in general, you can change the way they treat you on the job. You can let them know you are no longer an easy target for their mistreatment.

Example #3: The Customer Who Wouldn't Take No for an Answer

Catherine is an outstanding sales rep for an office products firm. She has won several awards for being the top sales producer at her company. She also works as a Big Sister on weekends and is in the choir at her church.

Yet when Catherine was sexually harassed several times by an important customer named Deron who wouldn't take no for an answer, she was accused of being too flirtatious by her district sales manager, who also told her, "Keep quiet about this whole thing. We don't want to lose a major account over something as insignificant as this."

After Catherine got this kind of negative reaction from her district sales manager, she wasn't sure what to do about Deron, who was continuing to call her in the middle of the night to suggest, "You want me—I know you do."

Catherine told me when she first came for counseling,

I'm not a prude and I can handle Deron's nonsense. But at a deeper level I felt violated as a human being. I like my job and I enjoy doing it well. But right now, with Deron coming on so strongly and my district sales manager treating me as though I somehow asked for it, it's extremely hard to stay motivated to do the kind of job I'm capable of doing.

In addition, Catherine's decision about what to do or not do was clouded by the fact that seven years ago she had been sexually harassed repeatedly by a previous boss and when she tried to press charges against him she was told by several colleagues that she would probably lose in court because she didn't have any clear-cut evidence. Her boss denied everything, and so she decided at that time to avoid the pain of a long, drawn-out legal case. She kept quiet for a few months and then quit her job because she felt so isolated and uncomfortable.

Now she was in a similar situation. She wasn't sure if she had enough proof to accuse this important customer. She knew she wasn't getting any support from her district sales manager. She questioned whether it was worth the bother to take action or whether she should simply quit yet another job because of sexual harassment.

Over the next several weeks, we began to explore in counseling two specific goals:

1. How to build up her inner strength in order to make a healthy decision for her career and her personal well-being

2. How to make sure if she did go forward with sexual
    harassment charges that she had enough evidence to
    be victorious

The turning point for Catherine came when she began to
keep a chronological log of exactly what had been happening with her customer, Deron, and with her unsupportive
district sales manager. Each week she brought in carefully
detailed written accounts of what these two men had said to
her in the past and were still saying to her in day-to-day
interactions that were hostile, demeaning, and unprofessional. After several weeks of keeping a running account of
their actions, Catherine realized she had more than enough
documented evidence to prove that something was terribly
wrong in this situation. She felt strong inside and she felt
justified in taking action.

With her attorney and a tremendous amount of support
from two of her close friends, Catherine made the decision
to proceed with a sexual harassment case. She was nervous,
of course, especially of what might happen if she lost and
her district sales manager became vindictive because she
was exposing his unprofessional treatment as well.

But to Catherine's surprise, the entire matter never even
had to go to court. When the top executives of Deron's
company learned of how much evidence she had compiled
about his unprofessional behavior, they were ready to settle
the case out of court.

In addition, when the top executives of Catherine's
company learned of the insulting treatment that the district
sales manager had given to Catherine, who was one of their
top sales producers, they transferred him to another division
and put him on probation while also requiring him to seek
counseling for his increasing hostility toward several women
he supervised.

While not every sexual harassment situation turns out this
favorably, there are two things that Catherine did that made
the difference between how she had been treated seven
years earlier and how she was victorious this time. The first

is that she sought professional help and the support of friends to make sure she kept clearly in mind that she is a competent worker who does not deserve the kind of treatment she was receiving from her sexually aggressive customer and her insensitive district sales manager. The second positive step she took was to make sure she did everything in her power to gather documented evidence, phone logs, witness testimony, and verbatim transcripts of conversations. She treated this sexual harassment situation not as though she was a powerless victim, but as though she was the healthy adult professional she indeed had become.

For more on how to deal with sexual harassment or gender discrimination situations, see Chapter 9, "How to Deal with a Testosteroni."

Begin Today to Start Writing Down What's Happening

If you have been feeling frustrated or victimized because of someone who has been treating you badly at work, for whatever reasons, don't wait any longer to start keeping a chronological log of exactly what's been occurring.

You don't need to decide yet what you are going to do with your written documentation. It might just be something to help you keep a clear perspective of what has been upsetting you at work. It might be the beginning of some constructive steps toward resolving the situation. It might be the basis of protecting yourself legally and financially.

Your task right now is simply to make sure you set aside a few moments each day or each week to spell out in exact detail what is occurring between you and the person at work who is getting on your nerves. Just keep telling the truth and putting it in writing. The truth, when documented carefully, can be a powerful source of clarity and action.

3

How to Begin Turning This Frustrating Situation into an Opportunity for Growth

Now that you've begun to describe in writing what's been happening to you at work, it's time to sort out exactly what you can do about it. When someone at your job repeatedly treats you badly, what are your options? What should you do or not do?

This chapter explains what causes some people to take positive steps to improve a difficult work situation and what causes others to do nothing or remain victimized. It will help you begin to make decisions about the best ways to respond to your particular situation in the most professional and successful manner.

The Case of the Dishonest Production Big Shot

I recently counseled a married couple named Nicole and Brian who are two of the most talented and hardworking people you'd ever meet. They've been married for six years, have two small children, and they work together as a scriptwriting team. They've written more than a dozen scripts together and sold several of them to production companies.

For the past ten months, Nicole and Brian worked hard to complete an excellent movie script about teenage pregnancy for a prominent television producer named Regina Stone. This project meant a lot to Nicole and Brian. They spent more time researching and rewriting this TV film script than they had spent on any of their earlier projects. Working without much income for those ten months, they expected a huge payoff from Regina Stone's company for the completed teleplay. Unfortunately, Regina Stone had also negotiated the rights to three other scripts on teen pregnancy. Her company then decided to produce someone else's script and to shelve Nicole and Brian's version.

Instead of receiving a lucrative payment, Nicole and Brian got a defensive phone message from Regina Stone on their answering machine. When the two scriptwriters heard the bad news, they had very different reactions.

Nicole was furious and wanted to lash out at Regina for her dishonesty and ruthlessness. According to Nicole,

> I just wanted to give Regina a piece of my mind. She pretended to be devoted to our script. She told us to drop all our other projects and work full time on this story. She said not to worry about the fact that we were doing this without a solid written contract. She said we'd done a terrific piece of writing. Then she drops us and goes with someone else. I'm not going to let her get away with this.

Brian had the opposite reaction. He claimed he wasn't too upset about what happened because he'd come to accept that in Hollywood no one can be trusted. He said,

> Regina isn't worth getting upset about. She's got a fancy title and a fancy car and a fancy parking spot at the studio. But her hands are tied. If her money men

say it's no deal, then it's no deal. There's nothing we can say to her that's worth wasting our breath.

These two opposite reactions—wanting to lash out and wanting to do nothing—are quite common when someone at work treats you badly.

Which reaction would you suggest is better for this situation? Should Nicole and Brian tell Regina off or should they keep their mouths shut? Or is there a third alternative?

The Three Reaction Styles

When an incident happens at work in which someone treats you badly, what do you usually do? Do you lash out? Do you walk away? Do you take some sort of appropriate action?

Based on my research and counseling experiences, I have found that the choice people make on how to respond to an incident at work fall into three types of reaction styles:

Rationalization and Denial: Similar to Brian's sense that it's not worth getting upset about, most people opt for rationalization and denial, which means trying to convince yourself that the person treating you badly doesn't really matter, or that the painful incident doesn't really hurt.

Burning Bridges: Similar to Nicole's strong feelings, some people tend to burn bridges, which means seeking revenge, lashing out, telling someone off, or making impulsive and irreversible decisions in the heat of the moment.

In addition to these two extremes, there is a third alternative.

Finding the Growth Potential: This third option is selected only by the rare few. It involves seeing the incident as a chance to discover more about yourself, more about the reality of where you work, more about the difficult individual with whom you have to deal, and more about how to be successful in stressful situations like these. Then you take action not out of denial or revenge, but in a creative way that maximizes your personal growth as well as your career growth.

Let's explore these three reaction styles as they apply to Nicole and Brian's situation. Take note of any similarities between their reaction styles and your own.

Style #1: Falling into the Tendency to Rationalize Too Much or Pretend It Doesn't Hurt

Have you ever let someone at work get away with treating you terribly? Have you ever been like Brian and pretended the nasty treatment at work was no big deal to you?

It's strange how many intelligent people roll over and play dead in work situations when they are mistreated by a difficult individual. Why do they pretend something painful or frustrating isn't worth doing anything about?

During one of our counseling sessions, Nicole and Brian agreed to stop for a moment and examine why they had selected such different reaction styles to this incident with Regina Stone. Beginning with Brian, we looked at what had happened to him in the past that made him so quickly slip into a sense of denial and resignation. Why was Brian so ready to give up and not do anything about this frustrating situation?

Brian explained that in the past ten years of trying to succeed—first as a free-lance journalist and later as a screenwriter—he had been rejected dozens of times. At the beginning of his writing career he had let those rejections get to him emotionally and sometimes he had become extremely depressed for several weeks before he was able to write again.

Like many other people who have taken risks and suffered rejection, Brian had made an unspoken decision to cut off his feelings and not let anyone like Regina Stone get to him on an emotional level.

In addition, Brian discovered in our counseling sessions that during his upbringing he had been taught not to make a fuss when someone treated him badly or when something was upsetting to him.

As the eldest child in a large family, Brian had learned at quite a young age not to let anyone see that he was upset or hurting. No matter how painful the situation, he thought he had to keep it all inside. Brian explained,

> In my family I was expected to help out all the time and not complain about anything. If I ever did get upset or cry about something, I got smacked and told, "Don't be such a baby."
>
> Even as a young kid, there was always someone younger than me in my family who demanded my parents' attention. My parents didn't have much left over for the older siblings like me.

As a result, Brian must have decided at a young age to keep his mouth shut and pretend he was fine even when he was hurting inside. In order to survive in his family, he learned that his hurts were no big deal. It seems Brian had been conditioned since early childhood to shrug his shoulders and say, "That's just the way it goes," even when someone strongly upset him. His passive response to Regina Stone's rejection and dishonesty was exactly what he had done for many years in similar situations.

Does this sound familiar at all to you? Were you also raised to keep silent when someone mistreated you? Have you also grown up to be passive and cynical like Brian because of years of putting up with unpleasant situations?

The Origins of Denial:

Brian is not alone in choosing the reaction style of rationalization and denial. Most human beings are in denial about how much they are hurting from being mistreated at work. They put on nice clothes each morning and they go to work. They get dumped on by someone. They smile and say, "I'm fine and I'm not going to let that get to me." They pretend it doesn't matter. They pretend it doesn't hurt.

But maybe it does matter when you are mistreated at work. Possibly it does bother you on an emotional level. Probably it does affect you on a financial level.

Why do people pretend a painful situation at work isn't bothering them?

When I've asked that question to women and men from a variety of jobs and professions, here are some of the responses I've received:

I can't do anything about it, so I just swallow my pride and put up with it.
It goes with the territory.
It's only a job.
It's only money.
It's not worth taking personally.

In addition, I've found in my work as a psychotherapist that when people pretend something painful at their jobs doesn't hurt, it is a form of denial very similar to what most human beings learned long ago as young children. For example, if you grew up in a dysfunctional family where someone (a troubled parent, sibling, stepparent, or guardian) attempted to put you down a lot or was mostly unavailable to respond to your needs, it's likely you learned how to survive by pretending this person's mistreatment of you didn't hurt too much.

Quite often, if anyone asks a mistreated child, "Are you all right?" the child will say, "Sure, I'm fine."

If you survived in your dysfunctional family by pretending that everything was fine, then it probably feels familiar and customary to deny your mistreatment at work.

A similar form of denial happens in childhood peer groups in elementary and junior high school. Can you recall as a ten or twelve year old being mistreated by someone and yet having to pretend it didn't hurt? Did you smile and say, "Sure, I'm fine," when in fact you were hurting inside?

Young children sometimes do the most vicious things to each other, and in order to survive socially they have to stand there and take it. Young boys occasionally punch each other, and even though it hurts, the boy is supposed to prove how tough he is by saying, "That didn't hurt. I'm fine. Hit me again—I won't flinch."

Young girls sometimes form the most vicious and exclusionary cliques in elementary and junior high school, often saying the most hurtful things to the young girls who are excluded from these cliques. Yet the excluded girls are supposed to pretend it doesn't hurt and say to anyone who asks, "Sure, I'm fine. I never wanted to be in their stupid group anyway."

A similar form of denial occurs in our adult lives when we get mistreated, yelled at, or excluded at work and we pretend to ignore it by saying, "I'm fine, it's no big deal, it goes with the territory."

So it's not surprising that Brian and many others have chosen to live with a bit of denial rather than to face the frustrations that they encounter at work. Denial is an attempt by our psyches to protect us from admitting just how difficult a situation really feels.

Denial is likely to occur whenever something feels overwhelming. We actually need some denial just to cope with daily life. For example, if it weren't for denial, how else could so many people live in Southern California? To live with smoggy air, on an earthquake fault line, with unbelievable traffic snarls, and then to tell our relatives back East that we live in the greatest place on Earth—that's denial! All human beings have some denial and rationalizations they live with on a daily basis.

To get through a typical week when you work with an extremely unpleasant individual means that you are probably doing a lot of rationalizing and denying. To paraphrase what one of the characters in the film *The Big Chill* said,

"Which is more important—sex or rationalizations? It must be rationalizations. When was the last time you went for a whole week without a rationalization?"

However, by remaining stuck in denial and rationalizations, you begin to suffer from painful side effects. In Brian's case, the costly results of his tendency for denial were:

- He sometimes gave up on projects or negotiations that could have become triumphs if he hadn't given up so quickly.
- He was becoming increasingly cynical and withdrawn, so much so that his friends were worried about him.
- Each time Brian resorted to denial and passivity, his wife Nicole felt more alienated from him and lost some respect for him.
- Whenever he fell into his habit of giving up quickly, Brian lost a little bit of respect for himself.
- Instead of taking time to learn the lessons from each setback or disappointment, Brian usually would dismiss the situation abruptly and not examine his options with any clarity.

Taking some time to examine why Brian was so cynical and passive in his response to Regina Stone was an eye-opener for him. Even though rationalizing and denying had been a lifelong habit for Brian, he realized in our counseling sessions that it no longer was his most viable option. Brian became interested in finding a more successful and satisfying choice than to simply resort to resignation and cynicism.

Have You Been Living with Too Many Rationalizations?

If you are like Brian and you've learned to cut off your feelings and pretend a frustrating situation at work doesn't bother you, then you might also be suffering some side effects from this habit of denying and rationalizing. Take a moment to think about the following:

- Have you said, "I'm fine; it doesn't bother me," even in work situations that are getting on your nerves?
- Have you resigned yourself to doing nothing about an abusive person at work even though there might be some constructive things you can do about this person?
- Have you isolated yourself at work, assuming that no one else understands your situation or can help you improve it?
- Do you find yourself rationalizing that the mistreatment you endure at work is part of the job, when in fact it clearly violates your job description or the agreements that were made to you when you took this assignment?
- Have you started to believe that it's just a matter of time before this unpleasant person forces you to move on to another job?

If you answered yes to any of the above questions, it is possible that, like Brian, you may have in your background some longtime habit of slipping into denial when you are justifiably upset, or of rationalizing too much when you truly need to start taking some appropriate action.

My advice to Brian is similar to the advice I would give to you: Don't get stuck in denial! When someone at work treats you badly, there are more constructive choices than shrugging your shoulders and saying, "Hit me, I can take it." You deserve better treatment from others. You are entitled to get a better outcome for all the hard work you've produced. Even if you've spent a lifetime backing down when someone mistreated you, this time you can change your response and begin to explore new ways of acting in a more professional and adult way.

Style #2: Falling into the Tendency to Burn Bridges or Allow Your Anger to Control You

Unfortunately, the only options that most people think about when they want to take action in an abusive work situation is to lash out, tell someone off, walk out abruptly, or burn some valuable bridges. Most people think the only choice besides being passive is to react with anger. So they fluctuate between doing nothing or doing something impulsive that makes matters worse.

Have you ever felt or acted that way? Have you ever thought that the only option besides doing nothing was to lash out or walk out in righteous anger?

I agree that it's very tempting to go up to the person who's treating you badly at work and say, "You pig. I hate you." But unfortunately, that isn't a very effective way to win friends and influence people in the work world.

It's also very tempting to storm out in anger when someone mistreats you at work, as if to say, "I'm mad as hell and I'm not going to take it any longer." Unless you own the company or are viewed as completely irreplaceable, that kind of righteous anger is usually a problem in most work situations. Especially if having an income is important to you or your family.

Burning your bridges and storming out of difficult situations are strong temptations when you know you are dealing with someone powerful who is extremely unpleasant or abusive. For example, in Nicole's experiences at work there were several instances when she walked out impulsively or verbally blasted someone who treated her badly.

As I stated earlier, Nicole is extremely bright and creative. Yet she had lost her temper at work during some unfortunate moments in her career. One time she got into a shouting match with an Academy Award–winning director who ordered her to be fired from his high-budget movie. According to Nicole,

> That outburst on my part felt great at the time, but it cost me a huge chunk of money and a few people who still aren't willing to hire me on their projects.

A few years later, Nicole got furious and walked out on an important meeting with a top executive from one of the TV networks. She recalls,

> I was technically right in walking out of that meeting because this executive was a control freak who was ripping my work to shreds. But in hindsight, I wish I had hung in there a little longer because that executive lost his job only a few weeks later and by then I'd burned my bridges and it was too late to go back.

In our counseling sessions, Nicole discovered why her anger was so explosive and, at times, out of control. She had not always been that way.

Nicole explained,

> When I was a little kid I was always considered a good kid, and my mother still wonders why I didn't stay that way. But as a teenager several things happened. First, I had to watch my parents get divorced and I was furious that my mother was so passive and powerless toward my father. The second thing that happened is that we moved out of a nice neighborhood into a much tougher part of town where I got taunted a lot by some of the kids at school. I had to learn to defend myself or else I was going to be swallowed up at that school. The third thing that happened is that my mother got married to my stepfather, who was abusive to her physically and emotionally. He also kept trying to hit on me and there were ugly scenes during those years. But I learned to stand up for myself and I'm glad I did.

While Nicole's anger had served her well in her teenage years as an important survival skill, it was now causing her problems in her work life as an adult. Learning to manage her anger and not react impulsively was a challenge she was finding difficult to achieve. As Nicole admitted during one of our counseling sessions,

> I take a lot of pride in my work and I don't like being treated like chopped liver, even if I am a lowly writer. But at the same time, I want to find some way to stand up for myself in corporate battles without losing my temper and alienating people or getting fired again. I don't want to keep walking out in anger or burning my bridges when maybe if I could control my impulsiveness I might be able to communicate better and keep my work relationships from falling apart.

Nicole's story raises an important question. How do you stop yourself from lashing out or walking out in defiant anger? How do you stay coherent and professional even when someone toxic is giving you a hard time?

An important customer is screaming at you. A business partner or colleague is being dishonest or manipulative. A supplier is making weak excuses for a late delivery. A boss or coworker is breathing down your neck. At times like these, you need a device for keeping your composure and your sense of professionalism. What I suggested to Nicole is a technique that has worked beautifully for many women and men who tend to react with impulsiveness or anger in stressful work situations. The technique is a simple device that can help you regain control over your reactions at exactly those moments when your anger or desire to burn bridges is beginning to flare up.

Counting the Colors

The exercise I recommended to Nicole is called counting the colors, and it's simple to understand. But you need to practice it several times so you will have it ready in case you need it during a stressful moment at work in which you feel the urge to lash out or walk out in righteous anger. This counting the colors exercise has three specific purposes:

- To prevent you from reacting too quickly and saying something that you will later regret
- To help you regain your best clarity of mind and your strongest ability to make excellent long-term decisions
- To make sure you don't withdraw into passivity or compliance, but instead have a tool for quickly regaining your capacity for standing up for yourself in an appropriate way

The steps involved in counting the colors should be followed exactly as described below. Here's what you can do as soon as you begin to feel your anger starting to rise or if you feel foggy because someone has treated you badly at work and you're tempted to walk out or lash out in anger:

1. If possible, take a short break and do this exercise in complete privacy. Go into an office, a cubicle, or a safe location away from the abusive individual. If that is not possible, you can still do this exercise and get equally strong benefits. While the other person is speaking or during a lull in the conversation, simply give yourself at least thirty seconds to do this counting the colors technique unobtrusively. Even while someone else is speaking, you can follow the steps listed below. Just do it silently and to yourself. No one will know what you're up to, and there's no reason to tell the difficult individual anything about this exercise. You can continue to look as though you are paying attention, but in fact you are doing a brief, silent exercise to control your anger and regain your clarity of mind.

2. Begin the exercise by noticing the colors that you can see in your immediate environment. What colors can you see in your clothing? What colors do you

perceive in the room around you? What colors do you notice on the other people in the room? What colors do you spot in the furniture, the carpets, the decorations on the walls, the items on the desk?

3. Slowly breathe in and out as you count from one to twelve and simultaneously say to yourself one color for each number. For example, without letting anyone know what you're doing, notice and say to yourself (without moving your lips):

   One—that's a blue shirt.
   Two—that's a silver earring.
   Three—that's a yellow pad of paper.
   Four—that's a green ficus tree.
   Five—that's a gold-plated pen.
   Six—that's a gray carpet with pink and red stripes.

   Note that you can repeat any color several times if you see more than one object with that color. If, for instance, you see a green plant, a green computer screen, and a green dress, they can each be given a separate number. The twelve colors don't have to be twelve different colors, just twelve different objects.

4. As you say to yourself the twelve colors and objects you see in your immediate environment, notice how your visual perception is getting clearer. Your mind is becoming more fully alert. You can focus more easily now. Notice also that the fight-or-flight response to your anger is changing into clarity of mind. Also, the foggy, confused feeling you previously experienced is now beginning to clear up.

   The reason this exercise worked for Nicole and many others I've suggested it to is because it reactivates the parts of your brain that get shut off when someone triggers your anger. The usual physiological response when someone upsets you is called the fight-or-flight anger response. When someone angers you in a work situation, your adrenaline surges and you feel like either lashing out (fighting) or walking out (flight). That's a normal physiological response to harm or danger. Your rational mind takes a nap while the more primitive fight-or-flight response takes over.

By utilizing the counting the colors technique, you begin to relax the adrenal surge in your body. You calm the fight-or-flight response by focusing for a few moments on soothing colors. Your visual senses are awakened and so are your rational capabilities. Instead of feeling out of control, you regain sufficient control to address the immediate situation with far more clarity.

5. When you have successfully noticed and said to yourself at least twelve colors, you can stop and once again take a deep breath in and out. You are no longer trapped in the fight-or-flight anger response. You are ready to find a far more successful and appropriate response to the person who's treated you badly.

Nicole did this exercise right in the middle of feeling angry about Regina Stone and the rejected script. She slowly breathed in and out for thirty seconds as she counted the colors she saw around her. By the time Nicole had reached the twelfth color, she felt a lot less agitated and a lot more rational than when she began the exercise. As Nicole described,

Looking at colors and not giving in to my usual way of reacting with explosive anger was pretty interesting for me. I noticed my eyesight became a lot less fuzzy. My brain seemed to be a lot clearer and able to sort out my options with less panic or anger. My blood felt a lot less rushed. I began to feel less out of control and more interested in coming up with a response that wouldn't harm Brian and me in the long run.

As Nicole's example illustrates, if you practice and utilize this counting the colors technique, you will find it makes you more alert and creative in stressful situations without causing you to slip into denial or passivity. The more you practice it, the easier it will be to benefit from this technique during the exact moments when you need it the most. Having learned how to take control of your own reaction style, you will then be ready for the third alternative— finding the growth potential.

Style #3: Finding the Most Creative Ways to Turn This Frustrating Work Situation into an Opportunity for Personal and Career Growth

Once they had overcome the temptation to react with denial or with anger, Nicole and Brian were ready to start finding successful ways to respond to Regina Stone. During our next few counseling sessions, we brainstormed together and came up with several healthy options. Our goal was to make sure this incident with Regina Stone became the beginning of something positive instead of a defeat or a permanent setback.

Here are some of the steps we came up with. Can any of these be translated into positive action steps in your own work situation?

Positive Action #1: Find Out Who Are Your Allies

One of the biggest mistakes Brian and Nicole made in their initial dealings with Regina Stone is that they failed to reach out to people who could help them. Quite often in stressful work situations, good people feel alone and unsupported. They assume that no one understands the problems they are facing or that everyone is too busy to help out.

In your own work situation, do you know who your allies

and supporters are? Could it be that there is someone else who has been mistreated in the same way you've been mistreated? Might there be another person who sees the situation the way you see it? Perhaps there is someone who knows about what you're going through because he or she has been through a similar situation in the past. Also, it is possible that someone in your work environment not only shares your feelings about the situation, but has the clout or experience necessary to help a great deal.

Some of the reasons why Nicole and Brian got mistreated by Regina Stone were because of how isolated and alone they were during the ten months they worked on their script for her.

- They kept their own agent in the dark during most of those ten months so that their agent wouldn't interfere in the "trusting relationship" they thought they had with Regina Stone.
- They didn't establish any strong relationships with anyone else at Regina Stone's company, so they didn't know if they had any other allies there who would argue for their project in an important meeting, or who would provide them with crucial information that Regina Stone might be withholding from them.
- When the bad news came that Regina Stone had shelved their project, they still were reluctant to talk to anyone in their industry about it because they felt ashamed and embarrassed at being victimized.

Like many people in a difficult work situation, Nicole and Brian allowed their fears and shame to keep them from utilizing the information and support that were available to them. Only after we discussed this problem in our counseling sessions did they begin to take the positive action step of finding out who are their allies and asking these individuals for help.

When Nicole and Brian started to reach out more and become less isolated, they found out there was a vice president at Regina Stone's company who loved their teenage pregnancy script and would have fought hard for it in meetings if Brian and Nicole had spoken with this person directly and asked for her help. While it was too late to do anything about the pregnancy script at Regina's company, Nicole and Brian did take this supportive ally out to lunch. Several months later when this vice president left Regina Stone's company for a prominent position at another production firm, she remembered Nicole and Brian's ideas from that lunch meeting and she asked them to develop a project for her new company. With a solid written agreement this time and a much better working relationship, Nicole and Brian developed an excellent script for this supportive ally.

Quite often in a situation where someone is mistreating you, there is another individual who could be your ally if you found a way to establish a stronger rapport with this individual. Rather than feeling as though the whole place is against you or that no one understands, find out if there are allies who do understand and who do care.

Nicole and Brian also found out that one of their writer friends was a former roommate of Regina Stone's. When they told this woman about their frustrating experience with Regina, this former roommate said,

> I wish you had called me when Regina was starting to treat you like that. I know how to get through to her and bring out the good side of her. I'm not positive I could have saved your project, but I've had experiences in the past where I called Regina and got her to be a little more attentive and decent to people she was treating like crap.

Once again, keeping secrets and being isolated had cost Nicole and Brian an opportunity to have a possible ally do some good for them.

Looking at your own situation for a moment, is there someone you could speak to who has some clout or influence over the person who is treating you badly? Is there someone who could explain your issue or defend your point of view in such a way that the difficult individual would be more responsive? Is there someone who knows the workings of the system extremely well and can guide you on what steps you can take to resolve the situation much better? Is there someone you haven't yet asked for help, but possibly the time has come to reach out and get this person on your side?

Positive Action #2: Learn More About How to Protect Yourself and Not Get Burned Again in the Future

The second positive step for Nicole and Brian was to find out more about what they might do differently to protect themselves and their scripts when dealing with high-powered executives like Regina Stone. What were their legal rights and protections? What were the possible remedies if someone like Regina Stone broke a written agreement or an oral agreement? What are the intricacies of negotiating with someone who is both a friendly, creative collaborator and at the same time a hard-nosed business person? What are the ways that other creative people protect themselves against ruthless or self-interested colleagues?

Nicole described their earlier mistake.

We were a little naive at first about how to protect ourselves with Regina Stone. Our agent had warned us not to give Regina's company any of our material until we had a solid written agreement. But Brian and I didn't want to listen to our agent. We considered Regina a friend who was on our side creatively. We'd been to Regina's house, we'd met her kids, we'd had lunch with her at the beach, and we'd had long creative conversations. We thought we could bypass the legal stuff and write this script on speculation until Regina got the go-ahead from her contacts at the TV network. Regina assured us that we were doing a great

job and that getting approval for our script was going
to be a breeze. So we didn't discuss too many legal or
contractual details, and as a result we got burned.

That experience of getting burned became the breakthrough that helped Nicole and Brian begin asking questions
and learning more about how to protect themselves and their
hard work.

Whether your own conflict at work has to do with a
broken agreement, a costly delay, a deliberate manipulation,
or an innocent mistake, there are legal steps and protections
that can remedy the problem. Whether your difficulties at
work have to do with sexual harassment, racial discrimination, age discrimination, or some other form of insensitivity
or mistreatment, there are proper steps to help you resolve
the current situation or protect you in future situations.

Your crucial action step is to make sure you find out
exactly what your rights are, what you need to do to
document or substantiate your claim, and what you can do
to get this situation resolved to your satisfaction.

- Find out if there is a seminar, book, article, information
  hot line, or referral service available that provides
  specific information to help you become more informed about how to protect yourself better at work.
- Find out how others in the past have been victorious in
  situations like these and what specific things they had
  to do to make sure their concerns were taken seriously.
- Find out what exactly would be involved if you do
  need to file a lawsuit or begin a formal hearing
  procedure about your situation at work. What are the
  likely costs and steps? What is the deadline or statute
  of limitations? And what are the forms of evidence you
  will need to gather?
- Find out if there are better alternatives than a lawsuit.
  Are there simpler and quicker procedures that will
  force the other person to stop treating you this way?
  Are there corporate personnel managers, a union rep-

resentative, a mediator, a grievance committee, or some other agency or group that can assist you in resolving a dispute like this?

In Nicole and Brian's situation, they were able to learn quite a lot more about how to protect themselves and they made some discoveries. See if any of these solutions give you some ideas for your own situation.

Nicole and Brian took two of their more experienced writer friends out to lunch and learned a lot about how to handle the delicate issue of combining business and friendship with someone like Regina Stone, who acts like a trustworthy friend but is actually a self-interested business person. Nicole found out:

These more experienced colleagues taught us how to set up formal written agreements with someone like Regina Stone without appearing to be distrustful or ruining the good collaborative rapport between the people involved in a project.

I had never wanted to bother with details like that because I thought it would interfere with my being creative or spontaneous. But now I'm realizing that in order to be taken seriously in my work I need to be both a spontaneous person and an extremely knowledgeable person about legal protections and getting things in writing.

Brian and I will still be nice people, but we're no longer gullible nice people who will get victimized by someone like Regina Stone.

Nicole and Brian also began discussing with their agent and an experienced attorney how to get the rights back to their teenage pregnancy script that had been shelved by Regina Stone. Working with proper legal advice this time, they were able to terminate the option agreement they had made with Regina's company and they eventually sold the script to a cable television firm where it currently is being filmed to be shown next year on cable TV.

As you can see, the incident with Regina Stone became a new beginning for Nicole's and Brian's career. Now they were far more knowledgeable about how to deal with potentially difficult people in their industry. Because they were willing to talk to a counselor, an agent, a lawyer, and some colleagues who had faced similar dilemmas, they became much better prepared to protect themselves legally and financially.

I urge you to do the same kind of information gathering and support finding in your own line of work. What specific people could you meet with or take to lunch who could teach you more about how to handle the frustrating situation you're facing? What specific pieces of information do you need in order to protect your rights better and not get mistreated? What specific techniques do you need to learn more about in order to become a better negotiator for your own projects and your own financial interests?

I have found repeatedly that you can't control the fact that there may be difficult people in your work environment. But you can control how much you reach out and gain support instead of hiding or remaining isolated. You can control how much you learn and grow as a result of this painful situation at work. You can control whether you react with denial or whether you react by burning valuable bridges or whether you get creative and turn your setbacks into opportunities for improving your own professionalism and quality of work. Like Nicole and Brian, I hope you find a way to come out victorious from a situation in which you were feeling powerless and victimized.

4

What to Do If Someone You Work with Is an Angry Screamer

Now we move into more specific examples of how to respond to the people you face at work. Let's begin with the Angry Screamer.

Is there a hostile or explosive person in your work life? What's it like working with someone so volatile, knowing that he or she can fly off the handle in an instant?

When was the most recent time you were shouted at by an angry boss, coworker, or customer? How did you respond when this person began to hurl verbal abuse in your direction?

"I Felt Lousy the Rest of the Day"

No matter how adult or mature you feel when you get up in the morning and go to work, all it takes is an Angry Screamer shouting at you to immediately begin to feel scolded and judged, like a child feels when confronted by an angry parent.

For example, Rosalyn is an intelligent, well-educated

woman in her forties who has been very successful in her work life, but she admits,

> Last week I had an awful day when several things went wrong and then an irate customer started shouting at me. I knew this person had no right to be screaming at me like that. Yet I still felt lousy the rest of the day.

Bruce is a thirty-four-year-old middle manager who has a similar reaction to an Angry Screamer he works with. He explains:

> I'm good at handling most kinds of people. But I have this new supervisor who gets so wound up by a missed deadline or a tiny mistake. He's got a short fuse and then he just explodes.

A few days ago, Bruce had to inform his explosive supervisor about a costly mistake made by someone in his department. According to Bruce,

> There's nothing worse than having to go to this guy and admit there's a problem. The shouting and the insults really get to me: "How the fuck could you be so stupid!" "I ought to can your ass for this!" "I'm busting my butt to get this project done on time and now you idiots have screwed it up!"
>   I know my boss has a drinking problem and that his temper tantrums are out of line. But I still don't have a clue how to respond to his outbursts without making him angrier or losing my job.

That Frozen Feeling

I've discovered from counseling hundreds of women and men on this issue that when someone at work is shouting at them, it usually causes them to freeze up and not know what to say or do. Some people describe their reaction as:

That frozen feeling

Getting all knotted up inside

Wanting to scream right back at this person, but knowing it wouldn't work because of the power structure in my company

Wanting to cry but holding back the tears because that's just not the way it's done where I work

Wanting to quit

Wanting to get back at this person for humiliating me over and over again

Do these reactions sound familiar to you? Exactly what happens to your emotions when someone at work is screaming in your face or glaring at you in a hostile manner?

The Hidden Costs

Most people try to ignore the Angry Screamer they work with and avoid getting too involved in an uncomfortable situation. Unfortunately, ignoring the abusive comments and angry explosions of someone you have to face day after day doesn't solve the problem. The angry person usually sees your passivity as a welcome mat that says, "Go ahead, step here. I don't mind." When you do nothing about an Angry Screamer, he or she usually decides you must be an easy mark and the next angry outburst should also be directed at you.

In addition, the toxic emotional energy from this person can begin to affect your physical and emotional health. Working in close proximity to an Angry Screamer each day is like trying to jog along a street filled with cars on a humid or smoggy afternoon. You can pretend the toxic fumes aren't affecting you, but later on you notice your lungs are congested and you feel sluggish. Even if you don't realize it right away, an Angry Screamer might still be destroying your health in subtle ways.

For example, here are some of the hidden costs of working with an angry or intimidating person that I've observed in men and women I've counseled.

Being screamed at and not knowing how to respond can give you painful physical symptoms. Some clients come into therapy with stomach problems, back spasms, itchy skin rashes, or tension headaches from working day after day with an explosive person. Others describe feeling depressed, anxious, or emotionally drained from walking on eggshells with a volatile individual at work.

Do you notice that you have specific physical or emotional reactions from working in close proximity to an angry person? Is this abusive work situation beginning to undermine your health?

Quite often the symptoms get worse when you know you are about to spend some time with this volatile person. For example, one woman I counseled told me, "I feel healthy and alive if I take a week off from work or even if I get a three-day weekend. But the night before I go back to face this abusive person, I either get a terrible headache or I begin to have stomach problems. Recently, the tension at work has become so unpleasant that I've been having problems with diarrhea and I lose my appetite for days at a time. This is no way to live."

Having an Angry Screamer nearby can increase the number of mistakes you make and can cause you to forget or misplace things that are important. What's your productivity like when an angry person is breathing down your neck or glaring at you from a distance? According to some researchers, the number of costly mistakes and workplace accidents goes up dramatically when there is increased fear and anxiety because of an authoritarian management style.

It's hard to pay attention to your work or to feel creative when someone is about to explode at you.

In addition, your short-term memory is hampered when your mind is distracted by an intimidating person. It can cause you to misplace or lose things or to have trouble focusing on details. If this is happening to you, you've got to do something about it or else the problem just keeps getting worse.

Working with an intimidating person can make you hate your job, even if you're in the right position and the work would be enjoyable if not for this abusive person. You know you can do the job and you've spent years preparing yourself for this level of responsibility. Yet if you are working with an extremely volatile person, you will probably begin to feel dissatisfied about your work, your career, and your future. Quite often the inability to deal effectively with an Angry Screamer causes people to dread going to work each day.

Many come into therapy talking about a career change or feeling depressed about their life in general. But in fact the problem is often that this therapy client feels powerless with a verbally abusive person at work and the frustration is wearing him or her down day after day, week after week. By learning to be more effective in response to an Angry Screamer, quite often the depression lifts and the need for a career change disappears.

Taking home the tensions from dealing with an Angry Screamer can make you increasingly impatient and short-tempered with your loved ones. One of the most troubling indications that you need to do something about an unpleasant situation at work is if it's spilling over into your personal life. Are you noticing yourself to be more impatient with your spouse or romantic partner? Are you more critical or short-tempered with your children? Have you allowed the Angry Screamer from work to verbally abuse someone you care about or to disrupt your private life with unreasonable demands? Are you becoming more sarcastic or negative because of this frustrating work experience?

I recently counseled a divorced woman named Amanda, who has two children from a previous marriage and works with a highly volatile colleague named Kurt. According to Amanda,

> When Kurt blows up at me at work, I often get quiet or I shut down and I usually don't realize at that moment how upset I am. But later on when I'm with my kids I notice I'm much more short-tempered and cranky with them. Or when I'm out on a date with my boyfriend Jonathan, I'm very moody, impatient, and not all that fun to be with.
>
> I thought I could leave my work frustrations at the office and not take them home with me. But having to spend each day working with a hostile person like Kurt is making me become someone I don't want to be. It hurts to think I'm putting up walls toward my kids and toward my boyfriend because I'm still tense from the situation at work.

Why the Volatile Person Gets Away with It

One of the most frustrating aspects of working with a hostile, explosive person is that he or she gets away with it time after time. The situation in many workplaces is that everyone seems to condone this person's abusive behavior. People might complain in the lunchroom or behind closed doors, but for the most part you hear a certain defeatist attitude that nothing can be done about an Angry Screamer. For instance, how often have you heard comments like these about a hostile or volatile person at work?

> He's a nightmare to work with, but the bottom line is that he makes this company a lot of money.
> She's impossible, but no one here stands up to her.

He's extremely abusive, but he's got everybody too
    afraid to do anything about it.
She's a very important client, so no one talks back to
    her when she goes into one of her fits.
He's a bastard, but so are most of the power players in
    this business.
I've been taking this abuse for so long I don't even say
    a word anymore.

When the rules of the workplace tolerate an Angry
Screamer and the people who work with this person remain
silent and compliant, the abusive person can't help but
conclude that the outbursts are perfectly acceptable. If an
Angry Screamer keeps getting raises and promotions because of his or her ability to bring in dollars to the
organization, then this person is actually being encouraged
to keep treating others in a hurtful way.

We've all witnessed work situations where someone was
rewarded for their bottom-line financial results even though
this person's mistreatment of people was way out of line.
For instance, fifteen years ago, before I became a therapist
and consultant, I worked in New York for Doubleday and
Company, first as a research analyst and eventually as the
director of research. I often did market research reports for
one of the division vice presidents who was extremely
explosive and abusive.

This vice president, whom I will refer to as Jerry Bark,
used to scream at his assistants and carry on like a madman
during high pressure situations. There was an inside joke at
Doubleday about Jerry Bark that went as follows:

Did you know that Toys "R" Us has a new wind-up
doll that's just like Jerry Bark?

You wind it up and everyone else shakes.

One time I asked Jerry if he was aware of how he was
viewed by most of the people he worked with. Did he know
how intimidating and harsh he had become?

To my surprise, Jerry smiled with great pride and said, "You bet I know that people are scared of me. I like it that way and so does top management."

Like many Angry Screamers, Jerry Bark was proud of his aggressiveness and had been encouraged by several raises and promotions not to change one bit.

What do you do when the abusive person you're working with is being reinforced constantly by a work environment that rewards aggressiveness if it leads to increased profits?

Knowing that I couldn't change Jerry's underlying personality or his obnoxious style in business, I nevertheless made sure to let him know clearly that he wasn't going to treat me or anyone in my department in a cruel or abusive way.

We had several skirmishes during the time we worked together at Doubleday, but each time Jerry came away from our interactions with a greater respect and more certain that I wasn't going to be one of the people he could mistreat. In fact, using many of the guidelines I will describe in the pages that follow, I managed to get Jerry Bark to treat me and my department with decency and professionalism.

Taking Action

Even if you've felt powerless and said to yourself, "There's nothing I can do about this angry person," I assure you there is a lot you can do. No, you can't turn an explosive individual into someone who never gets angry. This person has probably had a temper problem since he or she was two years old. Nor can you expect overnight changes in someone whose aggressiveness is seen by many as an asset, so don't expect this person to instantly become a gentle angel.

But you can alter the way you experience this person's abusive behavior and dramatically improve the way you interact with an Angry Screamer. Even if the other person doesn't change very much in terms of being a difficult individual, you can still make tremendous progress in changing the way you and this person interact at work.

Let's begin not by trying to change the other person but by changing the way this person's angry outbursts affect your emotions and your clarity of mind.

Action Step #1: Protecting Yourself If Someone Attacks You Verbally

Too often people wait for days, weeks, or months before doing anything about the pain that is caused by an Angry Screamer verbally attacking them in a work situation. You get screamed at in front of your colleagues and because you're at work you don't have an outlet for the pain and frustration you feel inside. Or you get shouted at by an explosive boss, coworker, or customer and there's simply no time to deal with the delicate feelings that have been trampled on by this insensitive person.

In order to regain your strength and be ready to take effective measures, you need to have a technique you can use right at the moment you're getting screamed at by someone.

I recommend three specific options that can turn a feeling of powerlessness into a recovery of your inner strength just when you need it the most. These three creative options are ways of using your imagination or your sense of humor to remain healthy. The instructions are easy to follow and they've worked for many women and men who were facing an Angry Screamer at least as awful as the one you encounter at work.

The Silent Mantra: Anyone who has studied meditation knows that one of the most powerful ways to relax yourself and stay centered in the midst of external chaos is to silently repeat a gentle word or saying, which is called a mantra.

I have a specific mantra I recommend that can keep you relaxed and centered even in the midst of someone yelling at you at work. As soon as the angry person begins to speak, repeat this mantra to yourself silently over and over again:

Hear the valuable stuff.
Ignore the anger. It's not yours.

No matter how insulting or loud the other person becomes, you can maintain your inner strength and your professionalism by staying focused and alert as you repeat this mantra.

If you practice this several times by repeating this phrase silently to yourself in the middle of a verbal attack by an Angry Screamer at work, you will be surprised at how much it can help you deflect the anger and allow you to separate out any valuable information you need to hear.

For example, Geraldine is a soft-spoken, sensitive person who works for a loud, explosive, and angry supervisor named Harold. Prior to attending one of my workshops, Geraldine was suffering from recurring migraines and several other physical symptoms as a result of working for Harold for almost a year. She told me during our first therapy session, "Either I have to find a way to deal with my boss or else I'll wind up in the hospital."

The first step for Geraldine was to develop a way to protect herself and not get destroyed by her boss's angry outbursts. Like most soft-spoken individuals, Geraldine didn't feel comfortable standing up to Harold or speaking up for herself. But she was willing to try the silent mantra I recommended.

For the next several weeks, whenever Harold erupted angrily, Geraldine repeated supportively to herself, "Hear the valuable stuff. Ignore the anger. It's not yours."

She discovered that

At first it was hard to keep saying the silent mantra because I wanted to get away from his anger. But the more I repeated the phrase "Ignore the anger. It's not yours," the more I began to see that Harold's anger is his own problem.

He's this driven, anxious workaholic. His anger isn't about me or my work for the most part. It's more about his own craziness that makes him so driven and high pressured.

Sitting back and saying quietly to myself, "Hear the valuable stuff. Ignore the anger. It's not yours," gave me a chance to slow down and stay relaxed even while Harold was bouncing off the walls. I don't need to get caught up in his craziness just because I work with him.

Every time I repeated the silent mantra I began to feel a little less affected by his anger. Lately I can hear whatever useful stuff he's saying that can help me do my job better and at the same time I pretty much stay out of the way of his angry tone of voice.

Keep in mind that this first step of deflecting the attack exactly when it happens is only a first step. There are more actions steps to follow. Yet this first step can make a tremendous difference in how well you take care of yourself and how well you will later be able to respond to an Angry Screamer.

Finding the Vulnerable Spot: A second technique for regaining your strength right at the moment of getting screamed at is a humorous device I call finding the vulnerable spot. To protect yourself and not get intimidated by an Angry Screamer, you can find and focus your attention on the most humorous spot of this person's appearance. Without ever letting the angry individual know what you are doing, simply catch a glimpse and then think about the physical characteristic you find most vulnerable and awkward about this supposedly fearless person.

For example, I have a huge bald spot on my forehead and happen to think bald spots are rather humorous. I especially enjoy having a private laugh at men who take one long strand of hair and swing it over their bald heads as if to convince the rest of us that this one strand can hide a huge bald spot.

So when I'm being shouted at by an authoritarian male, I

usually look for his bald spot and I focus my attention on that vulnerable part of his appearance. It's all done silently and I would never want the other person to know exactly why I'm remaining so calm and relaxed in the middle of a verbal assault. But instead of feeling intimidated or afraid of this guy's angry outburst, I usually feel a renewed sense of inner strength from knowing this bald individual is probably more insecure about his looks than I am.

I once counseled a woman named Laureen who used a similar technique when she was dealing with an explosive female colleague named Judith.

According to Laureen,

> I used to cringe and feel so powerless when my colleague Judith would lose her temper and yell at me over a crisis at work.
>
> But then I tried this humor technique and focused my attention on Judith's chin. Judith has the silliest chin. I swear she does. It makes me laugh just to think about it. It's rather wide and sticks out like Jay Leno's chin. It's almost like a TV tray table you can put food on and eat off of while you're watching TV.
>
> Whenever Judith starts yelling at me, I look closely at her chin and I feel a lot more relaxed and confident using this technique. She can make all the noise she wants, but I don't have to be afraid of her—not with that silly chin of hers.

I recommend that you try this technique with an Angry Screamer in your work environment and see if it helps. The instructions are as follows:

- During a quiet moment at work, look over and decide what is the funniest thing about this Angry Screamer you work with. Is there something about this person's physical appearance, way of moving, or way of speaking that is quite vulnerable or humorous?

- As you think about this vulnerable spot on the other person, remember to breathe calmly in and out. Relax yourself as you consider the fact that even the most intimidating individuals are extremely awkward and vulnerable in certain ways.
- Then, whenever this person begins to shout at you, remember to secretly find and focus on his or her vulnerable spot. Instead of feeling intimidated, you may begin to feel relieved or compassionate that the other person is a lot more vulnerable and awkward in some ways than you are.

Getting Immediate Support from Your Official-Looking Personal Journal: A third successful way to deflect the verbal abuse of an Angry Screamer as soon as it happens is to use a personal journal. Please note that this official-looking personal journal technique is different and separate from the chronological log and documentation that was discussed in Chapter 2. Most people use the personal journal for handling an Angry Screamer's cruel attacks as soon as they happen, while they later sit down and write up the incident in a separate notebook for documentation purposes.

What exactly is an official-looking personal journal? It is a simple notebook or pad of paper on which you can immediately write out your anger or frustration after someone yells at you. As anyone who has kept a personal journal can tell you, there is something very healing and empowering about writing down your resentments and emotions as soon as possible after an upsetting incident.

You should write in your journal either while the other person is still fuming, or if you need privacy you can wait a few seconds and take a coffee break or a rest room visit, where you can write out your feelings without being disturbed.

But there's an important trick that can make journal-writing far more successful in a work environment.

The trick is to make sure you select a personal journal that looks like you're doing job-related activities and doesn't cause anyone to suspect you're writing out your personal feelings and frustrations.

In most offices and work environments, it's inappropriate to be writing in a personal journal in the middle of a busy workday. So what can you do to write out your immediate feelings after a verbal attack from an Angry Screamer? How do you begin the process of recovery without having to wait and hold all your emotions inside?

Decide ahead of time exactly what kind of writing device looks appropriate for job-related tasks where you work. If you work in an office where people use spiral notebooks to do their jobs, then make your personal journal an official-looking spiral notebook. If yellow legal pads are the norm where you work, make your personal journal an official-looking yellow legal pad. If there is a certain kind of ledger paper, graph paper, or drafting paper that is customary in your job, use that kind of paper as your official-looking personal journal.

The key is to be able to write out your frustrations and upset feelings as soon as possible without having anyone suspect that you are doing anything except being busy at your job. Most importantly, to insure your privacy you may need to tear up and throw away your angry words or strong feelings after you've written them down.

For example, Kate works as a third-year attorney for a large law firm where,

> Not only are there some Angry Screamer men but also some explosive and verbally brutal women, including the female senior partner I report to.
>
> Last week this female partner was upset about an important client that we were losing and then she discovered that I was scheduled to take my vacation next week. Well, she went nuts! She started screaming at me for not being a team player and blaming me for everything that's going wrong.

In the past she usually would call me into her office and close the door before going into one of her tirades. But this time she started screaming at me right in front of several other partners. I felt so humiliated.

When Kate had first come for counseling four months earlier, she had serious stomach problems and headaches from working with so many volatile individuals at her law firm. But over a period of several months, Kate had become a lot healthier from learning how to use the silent mantra and the finding the vulnerable spot techniques to deflect the anger of those she worked with.

But this incident of being screamed at over her scheduled vacation was extra challenging for Kate. She admits,

As soon as this senior partner started accusing me of not being a team player, I started feeling guilty. I had made sure to schedule an incredible vacation after working so hard for so many months. I needed to go on this vacation very much and I was terrified that this furious partner was going to force me to cancel it. Or else I was going to lose all my status at the firm because I was being publicly reprimanded for not being a team player.

Fortunately, Kate immediately began to sort out her feelings, using a yellow legal pad that looked like she was doing official law firm business. On the legal pad, Kate began writing out her feelings of resentment and guilt so she could get her clarity back and not be destroyed by what had just happened.

Some of the things she wrote to the senior partner who had screamed at her were:

I hate you! You bitch!
You have no right to talk to me like that!
I am definitely a team player. I'm just not a sick workaholic like you are.

Don't you ever talk to me that way again in front of so
    many people.
I have every right to enjoy my vacation and I'm not
    going to let you intimidate me into canceling it.

To herself, Kate wrote,

You don't have to apologize for taking a vacation that
    you're entitled to take.
You are a team player and just because she accuses you
    of not being one doesn't make it so.
This storm will pass and once again people will
    remember that you've been doing a great job here.
Just remember to focus on what you can change and
    don't get overwhelmed by what you can't change.

Within several minutes, Kate had regained her composure and her self-confidence. She tore up and threw away
the pages of the yellow legal pad that had these statements
on them. Then she walked back into the office of the senior
partner who had yelled at her, and Kate suggested that the
two of them make a list of exactly how they were going to
get the work load handled during Kate's vacation. Instead of
feeling and acting like a victim, Kate had used her official-
looking personal journal to ventilate her upset feelings and
regain her sense of professionalism and competence. She
had regained her ability to think clearly again.
As Kate explains,

Several months ago I would have been emotionally
wrecked for the rest of the day because of an incident
like that. Being screamed at in front of people I care
about would have been just too much to handle.

But now I have some ways to get my strength back
quickly and not let myself become a victim. Writing in
my journal exactly how much I hate this senior partner
when she yells at me is the quickest way I know to get
the hurt feelings up and out of my system.

Then, after writing some positive and encouraging comments to myself, I was able to get through some of the guilt about taking a vacation. Instead of apologizing for taking a week off, I made sure I acted like a professional. I went right back into the senior partner's office and acted like a competent manager as I made suggestions on how we could best delegate the work load during my absence.

By that time the senior partner had cooled off a bit and she was actually quite pleased to see I had thought through how to handle the various cases I was working on. She pretty much agreed with most of my suggestions, and even on the ones where we disagreed she wasn't yelling or abusive any longer. I think it was because I had taken charge and not gone in there apologizing. I used my journal to get my strength back and I made sure this senior partner saw me as a strong woman and not as a weak victim.

To begin using an official-looking personal journal after your clashes with an Angry Screamer, here are some guidelines to follow:

- Decide exactly what kind of writing notebook or pad looks most appropriate for your work setting.
- Begin to use your personal journal at work for a variety of situations. When you feel tired or bored, use the journal to explore your feelings and regain your enthusiasm. When you feel blocked creatively, use the personal journal to draw, brainstorm, doodle, or describe your emotions until the creative urge returns for you. Most importantly, whenever you feel frustrated, angry, mistreated, or upset by something at work, use the personal journal to explore your emotions without censoring or inhibiting them.
- Make sure that if you write something that you don't want others to see, tear it up and throw it away. The personal journal works best if you know you can write

your honest feelings in it without ever having to show
it to anyone or be judged by anyone.
- Start today and see how much you can regain your
strength by writing out your feelings immediately after
an Angry Screamer yells.

Action Step #2: Finding the Right Words at the Exact Moment When You Are Being Confronted by an Angry Screamer

When someone shouts at you at work, are you good at
responding immediately in an appropriate and successful
way? Do the right words come to you or do you find
yourself saying too much or too little?

If you are like most people, your responses and comeback
lines might be a little delayed. I recall a woman I counseled
who told me,

> The trouble is that I stand there dumbfounded while
> I'm being yelled at and I have no idea what to say or
> do. Then, an hour after or maybe later that night when
> I'm trying to fall asleep, a great comeback line enters
> my brain. But it's too late. What good is a comeback
> line if you never have it at the moment you need it?

From hearing the experiences of many people who have
attempted to stand up for themselves with an Angry
Screamer at work, I have found that there are three specific
things you can say that are most effective. I will describe
these three options to you, and only you can decide which
feels most comfortable and appropriate for you and your
particular work situation.

The three choices of what is most professional and
successful when dealing with an Angry Screamer are:

Comeback Line A: "*Stop! I don't appreciate being talked
to like this.*" This assertive and straightforward sentence has
worked for many women and men in stressful work situa-

tions. It doesn't waste a lot of time criticizing the other person, which only makes him or her more defensive and angry. Nor does it waste a lot of time having you be apologetic or overly cautious.

In a simple and direct way, the statement "Stop! I don't appreciate being talked to like this," announces to the angry individual that you are a person with self-respect and professionalism. It lets the volatile person know that you won't permit him or her to walk all over you. Nor will the other person continue to see you as a victim when you stand up for yourself in a strong but nonthreatening way like this.

One illustration of how to use an assertive statement like "Stop! I don't appreciate being talked to like this" (even if you feel intimidated or unsure of yourself) is the example of one of my counseling clients, whose name is Douglas.

Douglas is a sensitive, artistic individual whose talent as a graphic designer has helped him establish a free-lance career that could potentially be quite lucrative. Yet Douglas has trouble with aggressive art directors and advertising agency executives who shout their demands and deadlines at him or who bombard him with angry criticism when one of his designs doesn't do exactly what they requested.

During his first few years as a free-lance designer, Douglas lost several important accounts because of his inability to deal with certain angry and intimidating clients. He admits,

> If I had been stronger or more effective at standing up for myself with a few of these high-pressure clients, I think I would still have those accounts and I'd be a lot better off financially right now. But instead, I have a huge number of debts, several projects for which I haven't been paid, and a lingering back problem from holding in all the frustrations of dealing with difficult clients.

What I discovered about Douglas from talking with him in counseling sessions is that, like most creative individuals, he tends to fluctuate between being too compliant with his clients and then being too impulsive in leaving certain clients who get on his nerves. If someone yells at Douglas at a creative meeting, Douglas will either say nothing and start feeling more backaches over the next several weeks, or he will give up on that client and abandon all the time and hard work he's done up until that point.

When I asked Douglas to experiment with the simple line, "Stop! I don't appreciate being talked to like this," he was reluctant at first to try it out. He said it felt a little too confrontive and strong for his taste.

Then Douglas lost two more important clients and he realized the time had come to experiment with some new ways to stand up for himself in a creative meeting or a business negotiation. So we practiced using the line "Stop! I don't appreciate being talked to like this" in some role-playing exercises in my office. Then Douglas tried it out in a real-life situation.

After working for several weeks on a design that he thought was terrific, Douglas went to meet with an ad agency executive who was short-tempered and verbally abusive. The ad executive was upset about one small aspect of Douglas's design and began screaming about how awful it was. Immediately, Douglas said, "Stop! I don't appreciate being talked to like this."

The angry advertising executive stopped yelling and stared at Douglas. The ad executive was surprised to have a graphic designer respond to him so firmly and succinctly. The ad executive asked, "How am I talking to you that you don't like?"

Douglas smiled and replied humorously, "A tiny bit too loud."

Surprised by Douglas's wit and self-confidence, the executive eyed him carefully. He no longer viewed Douglas as someone he could push around so easily. The advertising executive then said to Douglas in a more playful tone of voice, "So, if I talk to you a little softer, will you fix the damn section that I don't like?"

Douglas felt victorious as he said, "Sure, if you talk to me a little softer I'll fix anything you want."

While this comeback line, "Stop! I don't appreciate being talked to like this," doesn't always get immediate results, it does have a certain power and a nonthreatening quality that tends to make bullies, intimidators, and angry business people stop in their tracks and realize you aren't a pushover. Just as Douglas found that it successfully caused his client to lower his voice, so does it often establish a renewed sense of professionalism and respect from even the most aggressive individuals.

Comeback Line B: "Time out! I want to hear what you're saying, but I've got to ask you to slow down a bit." This second statement is a little gentler and much more specific. People who feel that the line "Stop! I don't appreciate being talked to like this" is a little too assertive often find that this second comeback line is far more comfortable and natural for them to use.

This comeback line is more like an invitation than a criticism. It states invitingly, "I want to hear what you're saying," and that can often make an Angry Screamer less agitated enough to stop shouting for a few minutes.

It also goes further to say specifically, "I've got to ask you to slow down a bit," which avoids telling the angry person that he or she is shouting. Too often when you say to someone who's yelling or shouting, "Hey, you're shouting," this person gets angrier and insists, "I'm not shouting, you're just too sensitive."

By saying, "I've got to ask you to slow down a bit," you sidestep that debate and you give the Angry Screamer a chance to see that by slowing down (and not shouting) his or her message will be heard much more clearly.

One additional factor that helps the line "Time out! I want to hear what you're saying, but I've got to ask you to slow down a bit" is the way you say the words "Time out!" If you want to use a little humor to relax the other person, then put your left hand facing down in a flat horizontal position with your right hand pointed up into the middle of your left hand to form a T like in basketball or football when the coaches or players signal a time out. Calling "Time out!" like this in the middle of an angry conversation or meeting can lighten up the mood somewhat and remind the Angry Screamer that he or she is dealing with an intelligent, witty human being rather than just someone to yell at.

Gloria's case illustrates the power of using this time out sentence with an Angry Screamer:

An intelligent and hardworking female middle manager in a predominantly male company, Gloria has had to learn how to stand up for herself in many difficult situations. But she admits,

> In my gut I'm very nervous about speaking up for myself or making waves. Even after years of being the only woman manager in mostly male environments, I still don't feel comfortable when a man raises his voice or tries to intimidate me.

Gloria was afraid to use the line "Stop! I don't appreciate being talked to like that." She worried about being called a bitch or being laughed at by her male colleagues.

But when she tried the comeback line, "Time out! I want to hear what you're saying, but I've got to ask you to slow down a bit," here's what transpired:

Gloria received a call at five o'clock one afternoon and was told to come upstairs immediately to an important meeting with one of the division vice presidents, who is known for being a real screamer. Gloria remembers:

> As soon as I walked in the door to his office, he started shouting at me about the rise in expenses in my department. Not just shouting but actually screaming at the top of his lungs about which expenses had to be cut or else heads were going to roll.

In the old days, I would have sat there and felt like a helpless child. My shoulders would get tense, my stomach would be in knots, and my brain would get foggy so that I'd barely remember half of what this vice president was demanding of me.

But this time, after practicing the time out comeback line for several weeks, Gloria was ready to be less of a victim and more like a professional manager. She took a deep breath, put her hands in a T like a basketball coach or a football quarterback calling time out, and then she told the division vice president that she wanted to hear what he was saying and so she needed him to slow down a bit. Gloria explains:

I don't think this division vice president had ever seen a woman call time out before. To my surprise, he did slow down. He carefully went over each of his suggestions and I got to respond to each one, telling him I could implement most of his ideas immediately and letting him know which ones I disagreed with or would need some time to put into operation.

From my calling time out and inviting him to slow down a bit, I think he got the message that I do care and that I do want to hear what he has to say. There was no point in shouting at me when I'd made it clear that I was a conscientious, take-charge kind of person.

Comeback Line C: "Let's talk about this. You go first and I won't interrupt. Then when you're done, I'll see if I have any questions." This third comeback line is even more managerial and sounds even more professional. Instead of being the passive recipient of someone's angry outbursts, this line gives you the chance to regain control of the conversation. By saying, "Let's talk about this. You go first and I won't interrupt. Then when you're done, I'll see if I have any questions," you accomplish two important breakthroughs with an Angry Screamer.

First, you stop seeming like a victim or a scolded child

and instead you become the facilitator/director of the conversation. By directing the flow of the conversation with guidelines like "You go first," "I won't interrupt," and "I'll see if I have any questions," you suddenly have more clout and status in the conversation. You begin to seem more like a competent professional.

Second, by letting the other person speak first and assuring him or her that you won't interrupt, you quite often can short-circuit the person's anger. Most Angry Screamers talk in a loud and hurried manner because they secretly fear they will be interrupted, outshouted, or outmaneuvered. They yell and hurry not because they are so strong but because they are so terrified that they won't be heard unless they yell and hurry.

By saying, "You go first and I won't interrupt," you sometimes can relieve the panic and fear of being interrupted that this person probably carries inside. You can be sure that the best way to get an Angry Screamer to yell even louder is to interrupt him or her. But if this person knows ahead of time that you won't be interrupting, it allows him or her to slow down and stop yelling.

Marla's case is a good illustration of the effectiveness of using this third comeback line with an Angry Screamer. A merchandising manager for a women's clothing firm, Marla often has to deal with highly volatile suppliers and customers. Recently she had to attend a meeting with an irate customer who in the past had brought her to tears with his explosive temper and unrelenting verbal abuse. As Marla describes,

> I'm good at my job and I can handle most situations, but this particular customer is so unpleasant to deal with. In the past he's been so hurtful and vicious that one time I couldn't stop the tears from streaming down my face. I was not looking forward to meeting with him again, especially since I was going to have to explain why one of our shipments was late and was causing his company a lot of headaches.

For several weeks, Marla had been practicing the silent mantra to avoid being overwhelmed by an Angry Screamer's hostile tone of voice, and she also had been doing role-playing exercises with me in which she used the comeback line, ''Let's talk about this. You go first and I won't interrupt. Then when you're done I'll see if I have any questions.'' Here's what happened when she walked into the meeting with her most irate customer:

From the moment I arrived, he was on the attack, screaming insults at me and my company, threatening to sue, calling me an incompetent fool.

There was a moment when he paused to take a sip of coffee. I stepped forward, and in the most professional and managerial voice I could muster, I said, ''Let's talk about this. You go first and I won't interrupt. Then when you're done, I'll see if I have any questions.''

I could see he was still angry, but that comeback line from me let him know that I was there to help him solve his problem. And most importantly, I could see him relax just a little bit when I told him he could go first and I wouldn't interrupt. From that point on, he spoke a little slower and he didn't toss out as many insulting comments.

I think what happens with an angry guy like that is he needs to know two things in order to start treating you like a human being. He needs to know that you're professional and he needs to know that you're there to address his concerns in a professional manner without minimizing or interrupting what he has to say.

By the end of that meeting, he and I had worked out several good ideas on how to fix the current situation and prevent it from happening again. But most importantly, I'd let him know that I'm a strong person and not someone who's going to lose my professionalism just because he's raising his voice.

Action Step #3: Uncovering Your Own History with Anger and How It Affects You at Work

Thus far we have talked about several effective ways to respond to an Angry Screamer. Yet you might still feel blocked or uncomfortable regarding this explosive or hostile person at your job.

Probably what you need is some internal work on how to handle the emotions that are bound to arise when you have to face an Angry Screamer at work. Quite often what holds us back from being strong or effective with an Angry Screamer is that this person stirs up some inner turmoil that needs to be resolved before we can successfully respond to this person's anger.

For example, here are four possible ways that your own personal history with the issue of anger can interfere with how you respond to an Angry Screamer in the workplace. See if one or more of the following sound familiar to you.

If you grew up in a household where anger was not expressed, you might feel as an adult that you don't have the tools or the experience to deal with an Angry Screamer at work. In many families, anger is suppressed, hidden, or kept silent. Family members would rather deny that they feel angry, even if it means walking around with a constipated grin on their faces, as if to say, "Angry? I'm nehhhhver angry."

If you grew up in a family where anger was rarely or never expressed out loud, how then are you supposed to feel comfortable in work-related situations where anger is right there in your face? It is as though you are being forced to learn a completely new language, one that was not spoken in your family of origin. Is it any wonder that getting yelled at by an Angry Screamer feels strange?

If you grew up with an explosive or hot-tempered parent whose anger terrified you, you might feel as an adult that you need to avoid or be extra cautious with this Angry

Screamer at your job. Many people who have tried to get away from an angry parent are shocked to find out they are working with an angry boss, colleague, or customer who is just like Mom or Dad. What a pain! If this angry person at work reminds you at all of someone from your past who was verbally abusive or intimidating to be around, that means you will need some extra help to make sure you don't simply run away from this stressful situation.

If you have an explosive temper of your own, you might feel provoked by this Angry Screamer and yet you probably realize that your own temper could get you fired or cost you in other ways. Quite often in a basketball game or football game, the angry person who provokes someone gets away with it, but the short-tempered person who strikes back gets caught. It's often that way in business as well. The Angry Screamer who starts the argument is usually someone that no one wants to mess with, but if you strike back at this person and lose your temper, you might find that lots of people feel fine about blaming the whole dispute on your unprofessional response to this person's provocation.

If you have felt mistreated in the past and you try to make up for all past injustices by lashing out at this current Angry Screamer, you might find your response gets you nothing but trouble. Only you know for certain if you are carrying resentments inside from past experiences at work where you felt an injustice occurred. If this is true for you, then you will need to sort out what happened in the past and what's taking place now so that you can decide on an appropriate and professional response to the Angry Screamer who is getting on your nerves.

If any of these descriptions sound like you (if you grew up unfamiliar with how to express anger, if you grew up terrified of an explosive parent, if you have a volatile temper of your own, or if you have been building up resentments for far too long), then you now have an important challenge in front of you. The challenge of working with an Angry

Screamer means that you can begin to sort out what happened in your past—why anger is such a difficult issue for you and how to respond more successfully.

I recommend for Action Step #3 that you take some time to do as many of the following as possible:

- Begin writing in your personal journal or talking with a supportive friend or counselor about your own personal history on the issue of anger. What was anger like for you as a child in your family or in your neighborhood or school life? Was anger expressed simply and directly without lingering resentments? Was anger kept inside or suppressed? Did anger in your family have such a painful impact that you still feel upset just thinking about it? Were there incidents in your neighborhood or your school life that made you uncomfortable with people who are explosive or volatile?

- Begin sorting out and discussing with a supportive friend or counselor what have been your work-related experiences with anger. What have been your triumphs or setbacks from having to work with angry individuals? What have been your good and bad experiences when expressing your own anger or frustration in work situations?

- Begin noticing your breathing when you are around an angry individual or when you are angry yourself at work. Are you breathing in and out slowly and evenly, or holding your breath out of fear, or breathing too rapidly and thereby feeling a loss of control?

- Practice ahead of time with a supportive friend or counselor how you might respond next time when you are confronted by an Angry Screamer at work. The more you practice how to remain professional and articulate during a confrontation with an angry individual, the more you will be able to convince this person of three important facts:

1. That you are not a pushover for him or her to scream at

2. That you are professional and calm enough to be able to respond to this person's anger without getting forced into his or her unprofessional style

3. That you can continue to do an excellent job and focus on what's important, even if this person is bouncing off the walls

Carla's story helps to demonstrate what can be accomplished when you see an Angry Screamer at work as an opportunity for you to seek professional help to resolve your own personal history on the issue of anger.

When Carla first attended one of my workshops, she only knew that she was upset from working with a highly explosive colleague in her department. What Carla didn't know at first is that this struggle at work was going to lead to major breakthroughs in her life.

I remember Carla sitting in the back of the room at the workshop where I first met her. She dressed in a professional manner but she looked tired and worn out emotionally, as though she were many years older than her actual age. Whenever she asked a question, she seemed apologetic and worried that she was going to get an angry response. After working for several years with an extremely controlling and explosive colleague, Carla had become very cautious.

Over the next several months in therapy sessions, Carla did some excellent work to find out why this particular colleague was so intimidating for her and what could be done to resolve her internal fears and difficulties regarding angry people in general. She discovered from her therapy sessions that

1. Because of her upbringing with a very explosive and intimidating father, Carla had a strong fear of being yelled at, especially by men.

2. Even though Carla was very intelligent, hardwork-

ing, and professional at her job, this fear of being yelled at was so strong that it made her foggy, forgetful, and mistake-prone when she was around this particular colleague who is an Angry Screamer.

3. This particular colleague had been treating her like a doormat precisely because she never talked back to him or stood up for herself. The more she acted polite and cautious around him, the more it seemed to bring out the hostile bully in him. He often would scream at her over a tiny mistake and blame her for things that weren't her fault.

By practicing in therapy sessions what she could say to herself when this colleague was breathing down her neck, Carla began to work through her lifelong habit of closing down when she was near an angry individual. She slowly began to realize that staying quiet was only worsening the problem. Yet it took her several practice sessions before she felt comfortable standing up for herself in a verbal confrontation with someone as explosive as this colleague.

A breakthrough occured for Carla one afternoon when this particular individual began shouting at her over a mistake that was not Carla's fault whatsoever. This colleague was upset about an important account that wasn't being handled properly and he was trying to vent his anger on Carla and blame her for the entire problem.

Carla knew immediately that this was a chance to try out some of the techniques she had been practicing in therapy. She first began by saying the silent mantra to herself. She repeated several times silently: "Hear the valuable stuff. Ignore the anger. It's not yours."

Then she took a deep breath and tried out the exercise we had practiced for staying professional and taking charge when someone is shouting at you. She said to her furious colleague: "Time out! I want to hear what you're saying, but I've got to ask you to slow down a bit."

That was the first time Carla had ever taken charge around an angry individual. She put her hands in a T as if calling time out. She looked her colleague straight in the eye and took charge of the situation.

To her surprise, this did get him to slow down and they began to discuss what could be done to improve things on this important account that was being managed poorly.

As Carla told me a few days later,

It felt terrific to see him slow down and start taking me seriously. I wasn't intimidated this time by his shouting. I kept my composure and I took charge of the conversation. After fifteen minutes of brainstorming solutions to the problem, he left my office and for the first time in years I felt victorious.

That began a series of breakthroughs in my life. I began standing up for myself with my ex-husband and my seventeen-year-old daughter as well. Using the same techniques that were helping me feel stronger at work, I began to let these other people see that I'm not a pushover. I didn't lash out at them or get hostile when they provoked me. I just kept my composure and knew exactly how to take charge of the situation.

Making Progress on the Issue of Anger

Since there are going to be times when an angry customer, colleague, boss, or partner confronts you at work, you owe it to yourself to begin working through your difficulties on this issue. Anger is a difficult challenge for most human beings; you are not alone in feeling uncomfortable when someone at work explodes in your face or attacks with verbal abuse that is hard to take.

I urge you to seize this opportunity. Take some time to practice the exercises that have been described in this chapter. Either with a supportive friend or a counselor that you trust, make sure you find out why it is that anger is such a difficult challenge for you. Take steps to become more competent and professional in situations where you are confronted by someone who's attempting to blast you with a verbal assault. Learn how to take better care of yourself during these hostile attacks, and you will become far more successful in whatever business crises take place in the future.

5

The Secret of Handling a Saccharine Snake

Have you ever worked with someone who pretends to be a caring friend but is actually an extremely selfish person who needs to be handled very carefully?

Is there someone in your work situation right now who pretends to be sweet and nice, but is actually working against you?

Welcome to the challenge of dealing with a Saccharine Snake. It could be someone you work for, someone who works for you, or someone you encounter quite often who is a customer, supplier, associate, or competitor.

When They Say, "Trust Me," Watch Out

A few years ago, Melanie Griffith starred as Tess McGill in the move *Working Girl*, which is about a thirty-year-old woman who finds out her boss is stealing the credit for her good ideas.

When we first meet Tess's boss, Katherine Parker (played by Sigourney Weaver), Katherine pretends to be sweet and very interested in becoming a supportive mentor for Tess.

Listen to what the new boss says to her assistant during their first important conversation. "I want your input, Tess. I welcome your ideas and I like to see hard work rewarded. It's a two-way street on my team—and call me Katherine."

For the first time in her career, Tess feels she has found a mentor and an ally. She tells her boyfriend (played by Alec Baldwin) how excited she is that finally someone believes in her and respects her. It's a feeling we all long for in our work lives—to be taken seriously and to know there is someone on our team who cares about us.

But when Tess gives Katherine an excellent idea for their client to purchase an outstanding radio station, Katherine attempts to steal the credit while assuring Tess the idea has been turned down.

Rather than being a supportive mentor or friend, Katherine Parker is revealed to be a manipulative adversary. Her sweetness is too saccharine. Her friendliness is an attempt to gain control.

When a Saccharine Snake says, "Trust me," it usually means "I'm about to do something behind your back that you're not going to like." When this kind of boss, colleague, or employee says, "I care about you," it often means "I want to take advantage of your niceness."

Does this sound like anyone you know? Is there someone you've been relying on who pretends to be looking out for your best interests while at the same time this person is trying to control you or exploit you?

Like strolling in a city park where people frequently walk their dogs, you might want to check your shoes to see if you've stepped in anything.

The Frustration of Being Taken for a Ride

If someone smiles sweetly while taking advantage of you at work, you need to find a way of protecting yourself. A Saccharine Snake not only can undermine your career success, but also affect you on a much deeper emotional level. Here are three examples for you to consider:

Snake #1: The Person Who Says, "No Problem"

Have you discovered yet that the words "no problem," when spoken by certain individuals, are a warning flag that trouble is coming soon? Joanne co-owns a small business and recently found out some surprising news about her business partner Steven. According to Joanne,

> Steven always impressed me as being an upbeat and hardworking person. We were close friends before deciding to go into business together.
>
> But recently I discovered he has been spending huge sums of money on himself and charging it to our business. I brought it up, and he kept telling me, "No problem. I'll repay the funds."
>
> Then I found out he has been taking days off to visit an old girlfriend while assuring me he was out making sales calls. Again his response was, "No problem— that relationship is finally over."
>
> Then I discovered that he's been covering up several bad investments he made and didn't tell me about. Again his answer was, "No problem." If I hear the words "no problem" one more time, I'm going to scream.

Snake #2: The Person Who Alternates Between Jekyll and Hyde

Have you ever worked with someone whose sweetness covered up a mean streak that was hard to confront because this person had so many others convinced of his or her innocence?

I recently counseled a man who works with an extremely controlling manager who tends to be vicious one moment while appearing humanistic and encouraging the next. The man I counseled explained to me:

> I'm never sure which personality my boss will show me on a given day—Dr. Jekyll or Mr. Hyde. It's

exhausting to have to work with someone who fluctuates between sweetness and cruelty. Even more frustrating is the fact that most of my coworkers and colleagues think my boss is an angel. He's real good at looking nice when other people are watching and then breathing down your neck when no one's around.

Snake #3: The Person Who Talks Behind Your Back

Have you ever trusted someone at work who says one thing to your face and another completely different version behind your back?

Life would be so much easier if we didn't have to deal with men and women who make promises they have no intention of keeping or who give praise they later contradict when you're not around.

A good example is from a workshop participant named Sheila who is an extremely hardworking, creative person and who told me how much she dreads having to do projects for a particular customer who is a Saccharine Snake. According to Sheila,

> I have this customer who says she loves my work and then I hear the next week that she's bad-mouthing me to several other customers as well as taking the credit for all my good ideas and insisting I didn't contribute a thing.
>
> Last month I did a project for this woman and she told me to my face, "I love what you've done here. This is wonderful. You're a doll!" Then two days later she tells a colleague of mine that she doesn't like the way I did it and would this colleague do a revision for a reduced fee. This is the third time that she's complimented me to my face and then bad-mouthed my work to someone I care about. I wish I could drop her as a customer, but unfortunately, I'm stuck with her.

The Early Warning Signs

If you work with someone who is overly sweet and manipulative, the sooner you face the truth about this person the better off you will be. Here are some of the early warning signs that you are dealing with a Saccharine Snake.

Does this person have a smile that is a little bit too forced or a chumminess that feels suspicious to you? Experts in the study of animal behavior have demonstrated that a smile is often more than just a smile. When a chimpanzee, for instance, shows its teeth in what looks like a broad smile, in fact the chimp is highly agitated, is preparing to defend its territory, and is making a hostile gesture to establish dominance.

This smile to cover up hidden aggression is also true for many human beings in work situations. The aggressive salesperson who smiles a little bit too much while twisting someone's arm to close a deal is revealing his or her evolutionary closeness to the chimpanzee. The boss, co-worker, or customer who pretends to be your best friend while secretly manipulating you is another good example of disguised aggression. Simply ask yourself, "Why does this person's smiliness or chumminess seem a bit forced?" You may find the underlying aggression easier to identify and deal with as a result.

Does this person surprise you with excessive praise or unexpected generosity just prior to when he or she needs something from you? I used to work with a business associate who had the strange habit of giving an unexpected gift or telling me how much he enjoyed our working together exactly one to four days before he would do something dishonest or extremely selfish.

The first time he gave me a generous gift and then acted dishonestly, I was surprised and not sure what to think. The second time he was overly sweet and then did something nasty, I was beginning to see a pattern. By the third time, I knew something was about to happen. If you start to see a connection between the overly sweet praise someone gives you and the selfish demands they make soon thereafter, you know you are dealing with a Saccharine Snake who needs to be handled very carefully.

Are there clues this person has left behind that will expose even the most talented cover-up artist? Sooner or later almost every manipulative person gets caught in a lie or leaves an important clue behind. If you are working with a Saccharine Snake, you can expect that at some point he or she will give you exactly what you will need to expose the deception that has been so difficult to work with.

Your task is to make sure you hear not only what is carefully scripted for your ears but also discover what is being said behind closed doors. The best way to get the complete picture about a dishonest boss, coworker, or employee is to find an ally who cares about the higher ethics or who isn't afraid to tell the truth about someone's games.

For example, when reporters Woodward and Bernstein were trying to uncover the Watergate scandal, at first no one would talk to them. Then they found a White House insider who they named Deep Throat and who provided them with important clues as to what was really going on. Is there a Deep Throat in your work situation who would feel glad to provide you with the information you need to deal more effectively with a Saccharine Snake?

Does the manipulative person at work insist on helping you when it's obvious this person's "helping you" is actually devoted to his or her own best interests? One of the ironies of dealing with a Saccharine Snake is that this person claims to be looking out for your needs at the very same time that she or he is working against you.

Unfortunately, a Saccharine Snake is often hard to refuse because this person knows exactly when and how to tempt you with promises you desperately need. For example, when a manipulative person senses that you desperately need a friend, a supporter, a financial rescuer, or some other crucial assistance, this snake knows how to promise you exactly what you are hoping to hear. He or she will make an offer that is so tempting that you will find it almost impossible to say no.

Going back to the movie *Working Girl* for a moment, it's important to remember that Tess McGill desperately wanted to find a mentor who would boost her career advancement. At her previous job, Tess had a male supervisor who promised to assist her career ambitions but actually was trying to fix her up sexually with his good buddies.

Being betrayed by that male boss was a low point in Tess's career, and she wondered if she would ever find a supportive mentor who would back her up for career opportunities. So when Tess finally found herself working for Katherine Parker, a female boss who promised to be the supporter and friend Tess had always hoped for, she truly wanted to believe these promises were true.

That's how it often happens when we meet a Saccharine Snake in a work situation. It usually comes at precisely the time when we are extremely hungry for the kind of support and encouragement a Saccharine Snake loves to tempt us with.

As you think back to your own initial contact with the person who you now perceive to be a snake, what was going on for you during those first meetings?

- Were you hungry for support and encouragement?
- Were you searching for someone who would say, "Forget all the others who didn't believe in your talent. I'll be on your side. I'll believe in you."
- Did this person give you a number of attractive promises about how this working relationship would be better than previous situations?
- Did something about those initial conversations strike you as being too good to be true, but you disregarded those doubts and trusted this person anyway?

- Did you have a secret hope that somehow this person would give you special treatment and take care of you like no one else in your work life had taken care of you?

How to Recover from Your Encounters with Various Snakes

Being mistreated by a Saccharine Snake at work can retrigger some painful emotions. It's not only the current betrayal that hurts, but also the deeper level of frustration that you have been hurt by someone dishonest in the past and now it's happening again. In order to be able to deal with this current snake effectively, it helps a great deal to identify when in the past you were manipulated or controlled by other individuals who were expert manipulators.

This Saccharine Snake at work is probably not the first person in your life who has said, ''Trust me,'' and then broken a promise or selfishly worked against you. When you think back to past situations in your life, either at work or in your personal relationships, has there been someone who resembled a Saccharine Snake?

- Did one or both of your parents have the habit of promising you things and then not keeping their word?
- Did a family member, friend, or lover in your past praise you with compliments one minute and then criticize you to other people behind your back?
- Have you ever been frustrated at having to deal with a parent, sibling, spouse, ex-spouse, or friend who was overly sweet and not very trustworthy?
- Have you ever been in a previous work situation with someone who pretended to be your good friend, but who turned out to be harmful or dishonest?
- Did you ever trust someone at a vulnerable time in your life and then find out later this person was not to be trusted?

If you said yes to one of the above questions, it doesn't mean there's something wrong with you. It simply means that you, like most human beings, have been deceived at one time or another by a clever individual. How you recover from that painful incident and how you respond to the current situation with a Saccharine Snake at work is your next challenge.

Specifically, there are two ways you can respond to the person at work who is pretending to be nice but working against you. These two options are:

1.   To see the current situation as one more defeat that makes you feel frustrated and powerless in a world where people simply can't be trusted
2.   To see the current situation as a positive opportunity to learn new ways to be more effective and get your needs met at work, even when you are faced with a dishonest or manipulative individual

Most people automatically fall into the first way of responding—to feel victimized and helpless against a Saccharine Snake.

However, I recommend to people I counsel at workshops and seminars that they treat the frustration of dealing with a dishonest individual at work as an opportunity to uncover and resolve some of the leftover feelings that are stored inside from previous battles with other manipulative people in their lives.

It is as though life gives us several chances to stand up for ourselves with dishonest people. Maybe in your childhood it was too difficult to stand up to a manipulative parent, sibling, or other intimidating person. Maybe in a previous love or work relationship you tried to stand up for yourself but you were unsuccessful.

Yet now as an intelligent and strong adult, you get another chance. Will you seize this opportunity to stand up for yourself against someone who is working against you? Or will you let yourself be victimized once again?

The choice is up to you.

An Example of How a Betrayal Can Be Turned into Healing

Even if your first inclination might be to give in and not do anything about a manipulative person at work, you can still change your mind. You can still decide to be stronger this time and try something different. You can work through your feelings of victimization from the past and make the current situation into an opportunity for growth, and possibly a triumph instead of a defeat.

For example, Kristine is an excellent teacher at a medium-size college who came to one of my seminars to learn more about how to deal with a manipulative colleague at her school. According to Kristine,

> This woman, whose name is Joy, gets on my nerves because she's so sweet and everyone thinks she's an angel. But in fact she's always spreading gossip and she tries to turn every situation to her own advantage.
>
> Last month Joy told me one day at lunch how much she admires my talents as an instructor and then two hours later she was at a meeting with the administrative dean trying to get two of my courses canceled so there would be additional room on the schedule for two of her own courses.
>
> That's how it always is with Joy. One minute she strokes you and the next minute she's trying to stab you in the back. Every month there's a different conflict between Joy and me. It's exhausting and it takes all the fun out of teaching. Lately, all I can think about is getting away from all this dishonesty and game playing.

Because she was so frustrated from her battles with Joy, Kristine was considering leaving the teaching profession and going to work in some other field where, in her words, "There's less office politics and no chance to get back-stabbed by someone like Joy."

Like many people who feel mistreated at work, Kristine was close to her breaking point and was considering a career change that might mean giving up years of training and hard work to get away from a specific difficult individual.

However, over the next several months, Kristine and I discovered during her counseling sessions that one of the reasons why the situation with Joy felt so overwhelming was that it resembled other painful situations from Kristine's past.

Specifically, Kristine had grown up with an alcoholic mother who seemed sweet and wonderful to outsiders but was frequently emotionally abusive to Kristine. Kristine recalls, "I could never convince anyone outside the family that my mother was anything but a nice person. Yet at home she was often cruel and vindictive."

In addition, Kristine had married at a young age to a man who also turned out to be a bit of a snake. She discovered, "My ex-husband appeared to be a handsome and loving guy who everyone thought was so nice, but in reality he was having affairs on the side and during our divorce he lied constantly about his financial situation. Always with a smile on his face, covering up the deception."

Not until we talked about Kristine's unresolved anger toward her saccharine mother and her smiling but dishonest ex-husband did she realize the similarities between them and Joy's deceptiveness at work.

As often happens with personality clashes on the job, Kristine's struggle to deal with Joy's sweetness and back-stabbing had felt overwhelming because it retriggered some of the old resentments Kristine held inside from her difficulties with her mother and her ex-husband.

During one of our counseling sessions, I said to Kristine, "It looks as though life is giving you another chance to deal more successfully with a manipulative person. Maybe it was too overwhelming to deal with your mother when you were just a young girl. And in your early twenties you didn't know how to outsmart your ex-husband. But now you're a lot stronger and wiser. Now might be the time to reclaim your power and not let Joy force you out of the teaching profession. Now might be a good time to resolve some of the feelings you've kept inside all these years about people who've mistreated you.''

As part of her counseling, I asked Kristine to write out a list of resentments she had never expressed toward her mother and her ex-husband. On her list she wrote dozens of resentments, including the following to her mother:

I hate you for pretending to be so sweet and kind when you were treating me so viciously.

I resent you for always putting your needs first and then trying to convince people how you were doing it all for your kids.

I'm frustrated at all the times I felt guilty for being mad at you because other people were telling me, "Oh, but your mother is such a sweet person."

To her ex-husband, Kristine wrote,

I hate you for all the times you lied to me about your love affairs.

I resent you so much for always making it look like you were the good guy and I was the mean one.

I hate you for all the times you smiled with those gorgeous blue eyes of yours and told me what I wanted to hear, even though it wasn't true.

I'm ashamed at how long I believed you when you were doing so many things to hurt me.

Then I asked Kristine to write out a list of her resentments toward Joy, the woman who was so difficult at work. Kristine wrote more than fifteen resentments, including,

I resent you for being so sneaky and always trying to make it look like you're being a good team player when in fact you're trying to stab someone in the back.

I'm frustrated at how many times I've felt like telling you off, but I kept my mouth shut because you have so much pull with the top administrators.

I'm upset that I've let you walk over me several times and made me dislike my profession enough that I've been thinking about giving it up after all these years.

Finally, I asked Kristine to imagine a visualized fantasy in which she would read these resentments aloud or tell off each of these people one at a time. In this fantasy, the other person can only listen and not respond except to agree with the things you say. Even if this visualization could never take place in real life, it can help you begin the process of healing.

While at first she was hesitant to imagine reading her lists out loud or telling off any of these individuals, Kristine eventually spent a few minutes on each person as she imagined fantasies in which she expressed her resentments to her mother, her ex-husband, and to Joy.

At the end of this exercise, Kristine looked and felt a lot stronger than when she had begun. She had released a great deal of unexpressed anger that had been weighing her down for many years. In addition, she felt stronger about not letting Joy take advantage of her the way Kristine had let her mother and her ex-husband mistreat her.

Kristine realized that standing up to Joy at work would be a lot less overwhelming than it had been trying to stand up to her mother or her ex-husband. Instead of leaving the teaching profession, Kristine now had the courage to face Joy's dishonesty more directly.

Your Own Inner Work

If you are like Kristine and you've been feeling over-whelmed or powerless to stand up to a Saccharine Snake at work, I recommend that you use a similar exercise. Either alone or with a counselor or good friend, do the following:

1. Identify who in your past was a Saccharine Snake, either at work or in your personal life.
2. Make a list of your resentments toward these individuals.
3. Imagine a fantasy in which you read these resentments aloud or tell off these people without their being able to disagree or respond except to listen to your resentments being expressed.

Even if this fantasy could never happen in real life, it is nevertheless an excellent healing exercise for your emotions and your sense of self-confidence.

Like Kristine, you will probably discover that the current snake at work is a lot less threatening to deal with than those from your past who were so overwhelmingly and emotionally difficult. You will probably be ready after doing this exercise to stop getting victimized at work and start taking appropriate action to stand up to a certain individual who is manipulative or dishonest.

Taking Action

Once you've made the decision to stand up for yourself and stop being mistreated by a Saccharine Snake, what do you do next? How do you confront a backstabbing individual without jeopardizing your own job security or your personal well-being? Here are some steps that I recommend.

Step #1: Get Your Supporters Working on Your Side

One thing that often happens when a Saccharine Snake mistreats you at work is that you feel alone and unsupported. Being betrayed by one dishonest person can also make you feel nervous about trusting anyone else. Especially if the Saccharine Snake was formerly one of your close friends or allies at work, it's difficult to reach out for support when you're not sure who else might turn on you.

For example, Colin is a sales rep in a highly competitive industry who describes how

> I was shocked to find out that one of my closest friends at work was stealing my accounts and bad-mouthing me behind my back. At first I felt totally alone and unsupported. Everyone thinks of this person as a terrific guy and I didn't feel as though anyone would understand if I said how upset I felt. In addition, I wasn't sure who else I could trust. If I couldn't count on my good friend not to steal my accounts, then why should I let down my guard with anyone else?

After Colin attended one of my workshops and began discussing his situation with me, we began to explore together who among his colleagues might also be a supporter or someone who could be trusted.

Whenever you get mistreated by a Saccharine Snake, it's important that you not dismiss everyone around you as being equally dishonest. While it's a natural tendency to feel mistrustful and to retreat into isolation, you need to take a few moments with a supportive friend or counselor to sort out who among your colleagues fits into the following categories:

1. Those you can trust to support you if you stand up to this Saccharine Snake.
2. Those you aren't sure whether to trust or not, but who might back you up if you tell them the facts and help them see the situation from your point of view.
3. Those who will probably side with the Snake for political reasons or loyalty factors you can't change, or who are too intimidated or disinterested to support your efforts.

In most work situations, it is like the fable of *The Emperor's New Clothes*. At first no one admits that the emperor is naked and that his new clothes are actually no clothes at all. They're too intimidated, and they don't want to make waves. It's easier to just smile and say the emperor is a great guy than to come out and admit the emperor is quite bonkers.

While at first you might feel like the only one who sees that the emperor at work is naked or that a certain person at your job is a Saccharine Snake, if you talk to several observant individuals you will eventually discover that many share your viewpoint but simply haven't stated it publicly. All it takes is one honest person to open up the communication and pretty soon many of the people will admit that, yes, the emperor is truly naked.

When Colin sufficiently overcame his initial feelings of isolation and he talked to a few of his colleagues, he discovered what most people discover when dealing with a Saccharine Snake—that Colin wasn't the only one who felt mistreated by this person. Even though no one had spoken up in the past, many shared Colin's view that this individual was not to be trusted.

Just as Colin did, I recommend that you take some time to consult with your colleagues and friends at work. Ask them:

- Have they ever experienced any of the problems you've recently experienced with this Saccharine Snake?
- Are they willing to discuss with you how much this person is costing each of you because of his or her game playing?
- Are they willing to brainstorm with you on ways to improve the situation without any of you having to take it on all by yourself?
- Would they be willing to back you up if you stood up to this person?
- Would they be willing to join you in a meeting to

confront the situation directly and offer solutions to the person who is causing problems for so many others?

When Colin asked these questions to several of his colleagues who also had their accounts courted or stolen by this individual, he discovered that several people shared his frustration and wanted to support him in confronting the individual. Even though Colin had assumed that no one else understood or would help, in fact there was a lot more support available than he expected. In your own work situation make sure you ask for support from any of the following sources:

- Colleagues and friends who work with you
- The employee relations department or personnel department or human resources department, if there is an understanding person there who has assisted others in addressing issues like this in the past
- A senior member of the company who is respected by others and who has the authority to step in and address important company problems
- An outside consultant, labor representative, or mediator who is familiar with the workings of your company and who has helped out in the past when there were clashes between individuals

Rather than assuming that you are alone in your frustration and that no one can be trusted to help, look again to see if there are supporters who want this Saccharine Snake to be confronted as much as you do.

Step #2: Finding the Right Words to Say to a Snake

Most people back away from any confrontation because they fear they won't come up with the right words to say. Some fear that they will be too angry or emotional and will jeopardize their own job security after saying too much.

Others fear that they will be too soft and polite without sufficiently standing up to the problem individual.

Which is it for you: Are you more worried about blowing up at someone at work or about holding too much inside and never making the impact you'd like to make?

To find the right words to use to a Saccharine Snake who has hurt you recently at work, I recommend the following guidelines:

DO'S	DON'TS
Be professional and managerial, even if the other person gets petty or nasty.	Don't wait too long to bring up the problem to this person. The longer you wait, the more this person will think that his or her tactics are working on you.
Be specific and constructive, pointing out exactly what this person did that was misleading or dishonest, and what you will need in the future in order to trust this person again and work well together.	
	Don't try to transform or "fix" this individual. He or she has picked up the habits of a Saccharine Snake for reasons that have little to do with you and a lot to do with this person's upbringing and experience.
Be prepared for this person to argue, disagree, lie, or manipulate without your having to get defensive or upset. Just repeat what you found to be unacceptable behavior and what you would prefer in the future.	Don't expect overnight changes. It may take five or ten direct conversations before this person realizes you are not being swayed and that manipulation doesn't work with you.

Coming up with the right words to say to a Saccharine Snake often requires a little bit of practice with a supportive friend or counselor. The reason to practice is to make sure you avoid becoming too defensive or verbally attack the other person. There's no point in losing your sense of professionalism or stooping to the other person's level. You can make sure you will be strong, professional, and articulate with a Saccharine Snake if you first do a little preparation to decide:

What is the one specific thing that this Saccharine Snake does to you that you would like to see improved? Don't present a long laundry list of gripes. Make your request short, specific, and constructive.

Even if you are dealing with an authoritative boss or an important customer, think of yourself as this person's manager or team leader. What specific behavior by this person would you like to see changed? The more specific you are, the better. The more you can focus on a clear-cut behavior and not on the person's overall personality, the easier it will be to avoid unnecessary defensiveness.

What are the phrases that will keep you strong and professional without making the other person resist your suggestions? Once you have a specific troublesome behavior in mind, how do you describe it in the most effective and managerial fashion? Here are some phrases you can use that help you focus on one specific behavior without making a long-winded personal attack:

> I want us to work together and there's something both of us can do to make that happen much better.
>
> There's a specific problem you and I can solve if we remember to . . .
>
> There's something that you do that I'd like to ask you to do a little differently in the future . . .
>
> There's a way you and I can improve our work situation. Are you interested?

Notice that each of these statements is more of an invitation for improvement than an attack or a criticism. Quite often the Saccharine Snake is an extremely insecure and defensive individual. He or she will respond much better to an invitation than to a criticism.

What will you say to this person if he or she does become defensive or tries to deny there's a problem? It's quite likely when you talk with a Saccharine Snake that this person will become manipulative, defensive, or resort to denial to avoid facing up to the problem you're trying to discuss. Don't be surprised or upset if this happens. It's standard operating procedure for most Saccharine Snakes to be evasive and elusive.

In response you need to remain calm, strong, and professional as you go right back to your specific points, repeating them as many times as necessary, using the same phrases over and over again: "There's a way you and I can improve our work situation. Are you interested?" and "There's a specific problem you and I can solve if we remember to . . ."

It is extremely important that the Saccharine Snake see that you are stubborn, persistent, and calm as you keep repeating your suggestions. He or she will find it much harder to manipulate you if you keep focusing on one specific behavior you want changed.

"I Kept Sticking to My Main Point and I Didn't Get Sidetracked"

You may recall that earlier in this chapter, Kristine was thinking of leaving the teaching profession because she was so frustrated with the office politics and dishonesty of a Saccharine Snake colleague named Joy.

In her counseling sessions, Kristine and I practiced how to communicate more effectively with a Saccharine Snake by focusing on one specific behavior and using statements that are an invitation rather than a criticism.

A few weeks later, Kristine called Joy on the phone and

arranged to have dinner with her at one of Kristine's favorite restaurants. Kristine explains:

> I wanted to make sure we met at a time and place where I was most comfortable, so I picked the one night of the week when I am most relaxed and I selected a restaurant where I knew I would feel comfortable, strong, and in control.
>
> I was nervous, of course, but I knew I was ready to talk to Joy face to face and let her see how determined I was to stand up to her dishonesty and game playing.

At her dinner meeting with Joy, Kristine avoided personal attacks and focused on one specific behavior she wanted Joy to improve so they could work better together. Kristine recalls:

> I was real persistent and kept saying to Joy, "I want us to work together and there's something both of us can do to make that happen much better."
>
> Even when she got sneaky and evasive, I kept sticking to my main point and I didn't get sidetracked. I kept repeating in a caring and nonthreatening way that if Joy was willing to make this small change we could work a lot better together.
>
> It took almost a half hour of her skating around the subject before she finally gave in and told me she was willing to do what I was asking.

Of course, that dinner between Kristine and Joy didn't solve the entire problem. Joy went back on her word three times over the next few weeks. But each time, Kristine would gently but firmly remind her of the agreement they had made at their dinner meeting. She would repeat her strong, affirmative statement of, "I want us to work together and there's something both of us have agreed upon that can make that happen much better."

Finally, after several weeks of persistently reminding Joy each time she broke her promise, Kristine began to notice a subtle change in Joy's behavior. She explains:

> Joy is still a pretty saccharine person. I can't change that about her basic personality. But with regard to me and our working relationship, she's very cautious now and she goes out of her way to make sure she doesn't say anything behind my back or bad-mouth me to the administrative dean. I've got several colleagues who are watching out for me on this matter and they've told me how much Joy is being careful to speak only in positive terms about me and my work. She still has the habit of bad-mouthing some of our other colleagues, but she no longer does that to me. That was my goal and my persistent statements to her have paid off.

Once again, this case illustrates that you might not be able to change the overall personality of a Saccharine Snake, but you can put this person on notice to make sure you change the way he or she treats you at work. Joy now realized she was not going to get away with bad-mouthing Kristine any longer, so she changed her specific behavior toward Kristine, even though she was still a bit of a snake toward some of their other colleagues.

Step #3: Let This Person Know Precisely What Your Limits Are

The toughest challenge for many decent individuals when dealing with a Saccharine Snake is that this person will take advantage of you unless you firmly and strongly say no to him or her. If you are the kind of person who has trouble saying no or setting limits with demanding people, then this can be a serious problem for you.

You will need to be extremely clear and focused as you say to a Saccharine Snake what you can do and what you can't do in response to his or her demands for favors at work. A Saccharine Snake will ask for the most outrageous and inappropriate things. If you say no to this person, he or she will try to make you feel guilty. Even if you know rationally that you have a perfect right to set limits and say no to a ridiculously selfish request by a Saccharine Snake, you still might feel unsure of yourself or guilty. One of the talents of a Saccharine Snake is to make people feel terrible for saying no to him or her. For instance, see if the following two illustrations resemble the struggles you've been having with a Saccharine Snake at work.

Example #1: The Case of the Demanding Customer Who Was Hard to Handle

Gary is the major accounts manager for a medium-size company who recently came to discuss with me his inability to deal with a demanding and persuasive customer named Justin who is one of Gary's most lucrative accounts.

Gary explained,

I am getting so worn out trying to keep Justin's company happy. They are so demanding and they keep asking for special pricing reductions and special service that we just can't afford to keep doing.

But my problem is that their buying supervisor, Justin, is such an incredible manipulator. He's taken my wife and kids and me out on his boat. He's bought presents for my secretary. He's wined and dined my own supervisor. He's incredibly persuasive because he knows exactly what to say to everyone to make them feel like he's their best friend in the world.

But in truth, Justin is a major bullshitter and his pushiness is costing us much too much time and money. We've got to cut back on all the special treatment we're giving him, but every time I say no or try to negotiate with him, he pours on the charm and makes me feel like I'm some sort of criminal for even thinking about saying no to any of his outrageous demands for extra service.

In his therapy sessions, Gary began to explore why saying no and setting limits was such a difficult challenge for him. Like many hardworking and decent people, Gary had succeeded in life by being agreeable and giving people what they want. While in certain situations this might be fine, with someone as demanding and manipulative as Justin, this was causing tremendous problems. Gary's company was losing a lot of money from doing too many favors for Justin's account.

Over the next few weeks, Gary and I began to practice exactly how to say no to people like Justin who refuse to be denied without trying to make you feel guilty for it. After several sessions of practicing how to negotiate with Justin and not give away too much in the negotiation, Gary was ready to begin setting some limits with this extremely persuasive individual.

The specific technique that worked for Gary was to say to himself in the middle of a difficult negotiation with a Saccharine Snake like Justin the following words: "The more I set limits with this guy, the more he's going to respect me."

This simple statement came in handy during the next business meeting between Gary and Justin. Here's what happened as Gary described it:

> I had to negotiate next year's prices and services with Justin's company, and to let him know which things we still wanted to offer as a special favor to them and which things we had to eliminate because they were costing our company too much.
>
> Immediately Justin tried to make me feel guilty. He started sweet-talking about how much he had enjoyed getting to know my family and me, especially the times he had taken us out on the boat. Then he told me this sad story about how bad things were at his company and how they might have to lay off some people if he didn't get some price breaks and extra service help from us.

I started to feel guilty, but then I said to myself two things that we had discussed in therapy. First, I reminded myself that 75 percent of everything that comes out of Justin's mouth is bluff or exaggeration. So I decided to stop feeling like it was my fault if they were going to lay off anyone, if in fact they were planning layoffs at all or if that was just another of Justin's bluffs. Then, I repeated to myself the line, "The more I set limits with this guy, the more he's going to respect me."

At first Gary wasn't sure if setting limits and refusing to budge was going to alienate Justin or lose his account. Gary was nervous when Justin refused at first to compromise his demands or be flexible. The next day, Justin sent basketball tickets to Gary's boss and offered to join Gary's boss and his family at a special autograph-session/postgame party with some of the players. Finally, Justin also tried to influence the negotiation by sending an expensive present to Gary's daughter on her birthday.

As Gary admitted:

It was getting harder and harder to keep sticking to what I knew was the bottom line in my negotiations with Justin's company. But I kept repeating to myself what we had practiced and said at least once a day the line, "The more I set limits with this guy, the more he's going to respect me."

Seven days later, Gary and Justin had another meeting and to Gary's surprise, Justin backed down and accepted the contract as Gary had offered it, with only a few small changes that were not at all costly to Gary's company.

Looking back at the difficult negotiation with Justin, Gary concluded:

I am so glad I didn't give in to Justin's bluffs and sweet talk and guilt-inducing garbage. I've never had to be this strong and stubborn before, but right now my company really needed to stop letting Justin's company take advantage of us. I've always been able to be a nice guy and give people what they want. But this time I had to keep setting limits and saying no even though Justin kept trying to make me feel guilty or foolish for standing up to him. I think he did respect me a lot more for sticking to what I knew was right and not being conned by his attempts to get me to back down.

If you are dealing with someone who is excellent at sweet talk and bluffing, you might need to do what Gary did. You might need to carry in your wallet or purse a simple line that you can look at and repeat whenever you need to hear its supportive message. Because when you're dealing with a Saccharine Snake who is willing to lie or exaggerate to get you to back down, you need to remind yourself that the more you set limits with this person, the more he or she will respect you.

Example #2: The Case of the Demanding Boss Who Pretended to Be a Sweetheart

Nora works as an executive assistant for a man named Burt who is extremely confusing to deal with. While Burt pretends to be a generous, kindhearted boss and is constantly talking about how much he cares about his employees, in reality he is terribly demanding and very difficult to work for.

Nora says,

Burt comes to work each day and says with this gushy smile that he is so grateful to have someone like me to count on. He cuts out little motivational sayings and positive-thought quotes from books and articles to share with us. He tells everyone at meetings that he is blessed to have someone as hardworking and devoted as me for an employee.

Sometimes all his compliments make me want to throw up because in actuality he is a workaholic and the most demanding boss I've ever had to be with. If I could find another job that pays as well, I'd quit in a minute. But I need to stay here to keep my medical insurance intact and I can't afford to leave this job for a lower-paying situation right at this time.

What Nora finds most difficult about her supervisor Burt is how he overreacts to every small detail and gets anxious about even the most minor issues. According to Nora:

The trouble with Burt is that he can't tell the difference between a pimple and a tumor. He gets into a panic if there's one person dissatisfied with anything that comes out of our department. He tries so hard to please everyone that he's a slave driver to work for. He's terrified that the entire department is going to get cut whenever there's the slightest rumor of a budget crisis or a reorganization going around. So he keeps demanding more and breathing down my neck over every minor detail. I don't know how I manage to keep my sanity working for someone as anxious and controlling as this guy tends to be.

When Nora came in for counseling, I asked her what might happen if she began to be more vocal with Burt to let him know what her limits were. Nora looked at me as though she didn't understand the meaning of the word *limits*. Like many people who work for a manipulative or highly demanding individual, Nora had never been able to set limits. She told me, ''I have no idea how to say no to Burt. He's so pushy and he expects that when he says, 'Jump,' my only response should be, 'How high?' ''

So for the next few weeks, Nora and I worked in therapy to help her boost her inner strength to be able to set limits with someone as demanding as her boss. We discussed why setting limits and saying no had been difficult for her in the past. Growing up with a demanding set of parents had made Nora always want to perform up to other people's expectations. In addition, with her husband and her children Nora had also found it difficult to say no. She admitted: "I feel guilty if I try to take care of myself or I don't come through and do exactly what someone needs from me. It's just the way I am."

But from working in therapy on her fears of letting people down and from realizing that people like Burt need to be told no or else they will just keep making unreasonable demands on her, Nora began to consider the possibility of setting limits with her difficult boss.

Then an incident occurred that motivated her to take action. Nora had been staying late four nights in a row to take care of a pile of work that Burt had tossed on her desk before he left town for an "important" golf tournament.

The next day, when Burt came back into town and told Nora he needed her to stay late to type a term paper for his son's college literature class, Nora knew for sure it was time to set some limits. She didn't want to alienate her boss or get fired, so she used a humorous comeback line with Burt that she and I had discussed in one of her therapy sessions.

Looking straight at her boss without hostility or victimization, Nora used a little dry wit and said, "Burt, I'd be happy to do your son's term paper, but I don't think you'd respect me in the morning."

Burt was surprised by her refusal and true to his form as a Saccharine Snake he began to pour on the manipulation. He told her how much he appreciated her work, how much he counted on her, and how desperately he needed her to do this for him. He tried to make her feel guilty. He tried to convince her that typing this term paper for his son was "the least she could do for a good friend."

Even though Nora was worried for a moment that she might be fired, she kept saying, "No, I'm not going to have the time to take care of that for you," and "No, I've got some important things to take care of for my own family tonight.''

She recalls what happened next:

I thought he was going to get upset with me or try to wear down my resistance with more of his gushy manipulation. But to my surprise, after my fifth time saying no, he stopped demanding. He looked at me as though he was seeing me for the very first time. He said, ''If you won't help out, then I'll just have to do it myself.'' And then he sat down and typed it himself. I was shocked. I had never told him no like this before. And I had no idea that he would listen to me say no and not try to get back at me for it. In fact, rather than retaliating against me, I think Burt has actually respected me a little more for standing up to him. He's still pretty demanding, but less so now that I've showed him I'm capable of drawing the line and telling him no.

Have You Said No to Anyone Lately?

For many people in work situations, saying no is extremely difficult. Many tend to feel guilty if they refuse even the most unreasonable demands. They try to be all things to all people. They would rather burn out and get sick than have to tell an important boss or customer the word *no*.

Yet you might find as Nora did that when you tell an overly demanding individual the word *no*, it causes that person to respect you a little bit more. He or she might protest a little or make you feel guilty, but if you start to say no to the things that go too far or are not part of your job, you will find that after a little bit of flack you will be respected a lot more in the morning.

I'm not saying that you should begin ignoring your responsibilities or that you should say no to something that is truly a part of your job. But if you begin to show the Saccharine Snake at your job that you will not be manipulated easily and that you will not jump every time he or she says, "Jump," then this person quite often will begin to treat you less like a doormat and more like a human being. Wouldn't that be a pleasant change of pace!

6

Are You Working with a Space Case?

Have you noticed that some people are so laid back they practically fall over?

You're trying to get a job done and you need a certain individual to complete his or her part of the task. But this person seems to be operating on only a small percentage of brain capacity. Your task becomes far more difficult because of this person's spaciness.

What would your daily life be like if you didn't have to deal with Space Cases—people who are unreliable, easily distracted, and hard to pin down?

Unfortunately, most of us suffer frequent aggravation from people who seem to be operating on a different wavelength.

On the West Coast, that can mean a secretary who tells you the memo is late and filled with typographical errors because "Mercury is in retrograde and the astrologer said nothing will flow smoothly until a week from Tuesday."

On the East Coast, that can mean a boss or major customer who shows up forty-five minutes late for a meeting because "My racquetball partner was telling me about an incredible bargain in the Hamptons. I hope you don't mind if I call my broker."

The definition of a Space Case is someone whose mind is easily distracted by anything except the work you need him or her to do.

"I Felt Like a Wreck"

In addition to the delays and foul-ups that a Space Case can cause you, there is also the stomach acid and frustration that is stirred up inside you when you're dealing with someone who is chronically unreliable.

I recently counseled a woman who works as the executive assistant to a man who makes over $100,000 a year but who is so spacey that he would be unable to function in business if she didn't guide his every move. The executive assistant's name is Lynne and she explained to me:

> At least ten times a day I have to stop what I'm doing and take care of some problem my boss has generated with his incompetence.
>
> He's really quite brilliant in the technical area that he knows well, but as for remembering names, showing up for appointments, or getting anything done on time, he's the equivalent of a four year old.
>
> Last week he was supposed to be at an important meeting with investors at exactly 10 A.M. I received a call at 10:25 asking if I knew where he was. By the time I tracked him down at his favorite research library it was almost 11:00. Fortunately, I talked the investors into making it a lunch meeting and I arranged for a great meal to be brought in on short notice.
>
> We got the investors interested, but by the end of that day I felt like a wreck. I don't know if I can keep it up much longer.

Another therapy client of mine, whose name is Lee, works in a high-pressure environment where he has to share a secretary with his boss. According to Lee,

I could do my job so much easier if I wasn't stuck with this Space Case for a secretary. Yet I can't fire her. She's my boss's sister-in-law and for some reason my boss thinks she's the greatest.

Last week she did something that epitomizes just how little she cares about doing a good job. I gave her an important memo to fix and then photocopy for several important people. Since she usually can't remember my telling her how many copies to make, I got one of those Post-It notes and stuck it on the memo with the words "Make 6 copies."

The next day I get a copy of the memo and I can't believe what she's done. She photocopied it with the Post-It still stuck on the memo. So everyone got a copy that has this Post-It right in the middle of the page with the words, "Make 6 copies" on it. If this was all she'd done it would be no big deal. But every other day she does something else that shows how little she cares.

What Lee and many others have found to be the most frustrating aspect of working with a Space Case is that this individual's lack of professionalism often reflects badly on you. As Lee describes,

If it was just a problem of this secretary being slow or a little scattered, I wouldn't mind. But so many times I have to rely on her to do something important with customers or colleagues in my field, and her incompetence makes me look like a jerk. I've tried to make sure that I don't entrust her with anything that can hurt me professionally, but I can only do so much to watch over her and every so often she does things that I know are hurting my credibility with people I care about.

Where Does It Hurt?

To make an accurate assessment of how a Space Case at work is affecting you personally and professionally, consider the following questions:

- Have you taken on extra work because this person has been unable to carry his or her share of the load?
- Are you running behind on some of your deadlines because this person is holding you up?
- Does this person forget to give you important information that you need in order to do your job well?
- Do you take it personally when this individual seems apathetic or disinterested about something at work that means a lot to you?
- Do you find it irritating that when you attempt to discuss work problems and broken agreements with this person, he or she looks at you like you're being unreasonable?
- Do you feel like screaming when this person brings his or her outside interests into a work situation and gets distracted from the work you need this person to do?
- Are you frustrated that this person is getting paid for not doing a good job, while you are getting no credit for cleaning up this person's messes?

Taking Action

To work more successfully with a Space Case, you will need to use a four-level strategy. Each level is important, and it's essential to have all four levels operating at the same time. The four-level strategy for dealing with a Space Case at work consists of:

Level 1:   *Document each incident.* This can help tremendously if you ever need to get this person removed, or in case you need to protect yourself against a wrongful termination or a potentially costly lawsuit.

Level 2: *Work with the Space Case on how to be more responsible, reliable, and efficient.* There are some creative ways to help even the spaciest individual to do a better job. The tips and success story on pages 117–120 will give you some good ideas.

Level 3: *Find out what this person does well and make sure you redesign his or her job to utilize those skills.* Instead of using all your energy to find fault with a Space Case, there are more successful ways to get this person motivated and productive. How to bring out the best in this person, instead of continuing to bring out the worst, will be described.

Level 4: *Expressing your needs and limits so that this person can't continue to take advantage of you.* Even if you tend to be a self-reliant person and you aren't comfortable asking for help from people at work, a Space Case is someone who will ignore your needs and drive you crazy until you ask directly for specific kinds of help. How to do this successfully will be explained.

Now let's look at each of the four levels in detail to make sure they are done effectively to handle the Space Case who works with you.

The First Level: Document Each Incident

Even if most activities at your job are done with conversations and phone calls, now is a good time to start finding creative ways to begin getting things in writing. When you are working with a Space Case who doesn't listen very carefully to instructions or who can't remember assignments very well, it's essential that you put things in writing. Otherwise, your verbal agreements are only as good as the paper they are written on.

Every time you plan an assignment or make an agreement with a spacey individual, get it down on paper to be mailed or faxed. Make a copy for the other person and also one for yourself. Be sure it's dated and whenever possible, get a written response from the other person to acknowledge that the assignment or agreement has been accepted by both of you.

Writing everything down accomplishes several important benefits:

You give the Space Case a helpful reminder of what's been agreed upon. This can serve as a memory jogger for when this person forgets the agreement. It can also be an argument resolver for when the person says, "But I don't remember agreeing to that."

For example, if you are working with a customer or coworker who often can't remember or stick to the agreements you've made, putting it in writing can help tremendously. Irene, for instance, is a self-employed landscape architect who found herself getting frustrated by some of the Space Cases she had to work with. She recalls,

> I would spend hours with a customer going over the details of the work I was going to do. Then when the time came to install the landscaping, the customer would often say, "I don't remember agreeing to that."
> I had to find a way to get things in writing without losing the warm, personal style I like to utilize. So I developed a simple system of writing each agreement down on personalized stationery. This has added to the warmth and style of my business, and more importantly, now I have a written documentation to remind customers of the agreements they've made. It has saved me so many headaches to be able to point to this person's signature and say, "Yes, that is what we decided together. Here it is in writing."

A second benefit of getting everything in writing is that it creates an excellent paper trail in case you ever need to prove to someone that this individual ought to be transferred or fired. Having each missed assignment, broken promise, or frustrating foul-up clearly spelled out in writing helps your attempt to have this person transferred or fired taken seriously. It doesn't guarantee that you will be successful in removing this person, but your reasons will be given a far more substantial hearing if you have each frustrating incident carefully documented.

For example, Barry is a manager for a medium-size company who was having a difficult time getting top management to transfer his incompetent, spacey secretary and replace her with the kind of professional assistant he desperately needed. When Barry began to put everything in writing, his clout with the personnel department and with a senior vice president was strengthened. Barry explains:

> I used to go to the personnel guy and to my supervisors complaining about this incompetent secretary and pleading with them to let me hire someone decent. But where I work they are so terrified of making a hasty move that they would rather let a situation drag on for years without resolving it.
>
> The only way I got them to take me seriously is by creating an extensive paper trail of each amazing example of incompetence by this secretary. I kept a file folder in my desk of each broken promise, messed-up memo, flimsy excuse for missing work, and spectacular foul-up with customers who were very important to the company.
>
> When the file got thick enough, I began discussing it with the personnel guy and some of the vice presidents. Two things happened: First, they seemed to respect me a lot more now that things were in writing. I think before this time they had thought that I was just a complainer and they didn't take me seriously. Now

that they could see each incident clearly in writing they were a lot less skeptical. The other thing that happened is that their usual slowness to act was no longer necessary because we were so thoroughly protected by all this written documentation. There was no longer a fear of firing or transferring her because we would definitely win in court if the employee ever sued. We had so much clear-cut reason to remove this individual and we had it all in writing with names, dates, witnesses, and costly mistakes.

A third benefit of getting everything in writing is that it protects you in case you ever get fired, sued, or mistreated because of the Space Case you are working with.

For example, Mia is an outstanding salesperson who unfortunately was working for an extremely incompetent and spacey sales manager named Dwight. Several times Mia didn't get paid her commission on a major sale because Dwight had forgotten to turn in her paperwork. A few times Mia lost important accounts because Dwight was so late in arranging for delivery that the accounts went with a competitor instead. On one occasion, Mia was close to a huge commission on a deal that was almost completed until Dwight happened to take one of Mia's phone calls during her lunch break and his incompetence caused that customer to select a competing firm.

Then, during a business recession, Dwight had to fire one of his sales reps. As he had often done, Dwight chose to hold onto several Space Cases who were drinking buddies of his. Even though Mia had outperformed each of these individuals, she was fired.

Mia had never been fired from a job before and at first it made her feel devastated. But over a period of weeks, she was urged by several friends to pursue a wrongful termination lawsuit. The only problem was that she didn't have any of her allegations in writing.

Mia spoke to several lawyers who said they would like to

take her case, except that each of her allegations against Dwight was based on verbal hearsay. Mia had failed to keep a written paper trail of each of the times Dwight had caused her to lose accounts, had broken agreements with her, or had given preferential treatment to someone who was less competent.

When Mia finally found a lawyer who would take her case despite the lack of written documentation, she hoped she might win, nonetheless. But after a long wait for her case to be heard, Mia discovered that her evidence wasn't strong enough.

To her frustration, the presiding judge told Mia that he regretted having to rule against her in this case because she seemed so clearly wronged. But he advised her that the only way she could have won her wrongful termination lawsuit is if she had been able to present much more detailed written proof of each of her allegations, copies of the sales transactions Dwight had undermined, and witness testimony to each incident.

I cannot urge you strongly enough to begin keeping a written file on the incidents when a Space Case botches your work. If you ever get fired or sued, this written proof could mean a great deal of money to you. Or if you ever need to get someone fired, these written files will be extremely important.

The Second Level: Work with the Space Case on How to Be More Responsible, Reliable, and Efficient

At the same time that you are protecting yourself with written documentation, you can also be helping yourself by helping the Space Case to become a more competent person at work.

This is tricky, however, because if you are expecting a spacey boss, coworker, customer, or employee to become efficient overnight through some sort of miracle, I'd say, "Don't hold your breath!"

But there are some creative and effective ways to make a difference in this person's life, and to improve the way she or he operates in the workplace with you.

The key is to find someone who knows how to get through to a Space Case. Most people at work get frustrated trying to advise a Space Case on how to be more reliable and competent. The more this spacey person ignores your advice and instructions, the more frustrated you become.

That's why in most situations I recommend letting someone else do the teaching. Not only does a Space Case pay closer attention if the advice comes from an expert outside the department or company, but there are probably better things you can do with your time and energy than to start lecturing a Space Case.

To save your own time and energy, I recommend finding a seminar, workshop, or consultant who can help this Space Case improve specific skills that are important to working well.

For example, if the Space Case in your organization is extremely scattered or terrible at time management, there are seminars to which you can send this person that might help. Or you can arrange for a time-management expert to do a mini workshop at your company.

If lateness or procrastination is a problem for the Space Case you work with, you might want to send this person to a therapist or workshop that gets to the psychological causes and remedies for why people are chronically late and why they procrastinate.

If the Space Case has trouble keeping promises and doesn't give his or her word seriously, you can arrange for a workshop on integrity, personal ethics in business, or keeping your word to help this person with specific guidelines on how to improve this crucial area of trust.

If the Space Case is weak at customer relations or company policy, you can arrange for a seminar on those issues.

Your task is to answer three specific questions:

- What are the exact skills that would help this Space Case become much less of a problem and far more of an asset?
- What specific seminars, workshops, and consultants are available, and how much do they cost?
- How much is it worth to my department or my organization to see this individual improve these specific skills?

While there is no guarantee that a particular workshop will change this individual, I have seen numerous examples of Space Cases who made significant improvements because their organizations took the time to invest in their professional growth by sending them to good workshops or counselors.

Not only does the person learn specific skills at the training or workshop, but letting this individual know that you do care and that you are investing in his or her professional growth also has psychological benefits for this person's motivation and competence.

For example, Gloria is the owner of a small company and she recently hired a new receptionist-assistant named Tricia to handle the busy job of dealing with customers, suppliers, and independent contractors who call Gloria's company almost daily. Gloria realized that

> The receptionist-assistant's job is crucial to the success of my business. So I need someone I can rely on. The problem I discovered about Tricia during her first few weeks on the job is that she can be somewhat spacey and disorganized. Yet I didn't want to fire her because she's very intelligent and she really does want to do a good job.

So Gloria talked to several business associates in the hope of finding some workshops for Tricia on how to improve her skills at time management, organization, and customer relations. Gloria explains,

I knew I was too busy myself to spend the time helping Tricia improve each one of those skills, so after asking several friends and associates for suggestions, I found out that there were two excellent seminars I could send her to that weren't very expensive.

Gloria then sat down with Tricia and told her that the company was investing in Tricia's professional growth because they believed in her and wanted her to succeed at the company. Gloria related,

I could see Tricia's attitude change a bit because she could tell I was serious about wanting her to succeed. I asked Tricia to take extensive notes at the two seminars—one on time management and the other on customer relations—because I wanted her to come back and let others know what we could learn from her notes about the two workshops.

After Tricia took the two seminars, she came back and made a presentation about each of them and how the advice from the seminars could be incorporated into their organization. Over the next several months, Gloria concluded,

I was glad to see Tricia using some of the skills and techniques she got from the seminars. Even though she's still a little spacey and disorganized at times, she's made a significant improvement. She's a lot more committed to her job, and she's much better at dealing with customers and how to set priorities and meet deadlines. I can see that she is trying to do a better job and I'm fairly satisfied that the two seminars were worth the investment.

The Third Level: Find Out What This Person Does Well and Make Sure You Redesign His or Her Job to Utilize Those Skills

It's easy to find fault with a Space Case. The more rewarding challenge, however, is to uncover what this person is good at and how to redesign the job so that this person will become more motivated and competent.

Too often in work situations, people get assigned the things they don't do well and they begin to feel bored, distracted, or overwhelmed by their jobs. Or someone takes away from them the projects that they actually enjoy and are good at accomplishing. Is it any wonder that many individuals start acting like Space Cases because they feel so disconnected from their work?

Your task in responding to a Space Case is to find out whether this person might be doing a much better job if the tasks were redesigned and refocused. In many instances, the Space Case is likely to be more competent and reliable, but only after the job has been redesigned with this person's talents and interests in mind.

For example, the story of Marlene and her supervisor Albert illustrates clearly how a Space Case can be turned into a much more motivated and reliable worker if a job is redesigned correctly.

Marlene is a thirty-two-year-old assistant manager who is perceived by many at her job as being a Space Case. Recently Albert was hired to supervise her on an important project. When he saw how unmotivated and easily distracted Marlene was, Albert began to resent her and he wanted to fire her for what he perceived to be apathy and incompetence.

Albert was unable to fire her, however, because of Marlene's years of experience with the firm and her close friendships with top management. Albert was frustrated and he felt victimized by the situation until he brought in a consultant to look at possible solutions.

Within a short time, the consultant learned some important and useful facts:

- The consultant discovered from talking to Marlene and several of her colleagues that she had not always been viewed as a Space Case. Marlene had been a highly motivated and competent worker until seven months earlier, when her job was changed. Marlene lost the projects she enjoyed working on and she was assigned several new projects that she was not adequately trained to accomplish.

- The consultant found out from Marlene that she was bitter about the way she had been treated seven months earlier and had not felt like working very hard ever since then.

- The consultant also learned that Albert's job was in jeopardy if he didn't get excellent results on this important project. Top management was expecting a lot from him on this initial assignment and if he didn't perform up to their expectations, he would be replaced by someone else, whether or not the problems were because of his own actions or because Marlene was failing to keep up her end of the project.

As in many work situations with a Space Case, Albert needed to find a way to get Marlene more motivated and productive or else he might lose his job.

With the help of the consultant, Albert and Marlene had several brainstorming sessions in which they discussed what could be done to improve the situation. Here's what they accomplished:

- Marlene finally got to ventilate her frustrations about what happened seven months before and why she lacked motivation at work ever since.

- Albert finally had an opportunity to let Marlene know how much he needed her best work in order to succeed at the current project that had so much riding on it.
- For the first time since they had been assigned to the same project, Marlene and Albert began to feel like allies rather than enemies.
- Albert asked for Marlene's help in drawing up a job redesign that he would present to top management. This job redesign consisted of Marlene regaining some of the aspects of her job that she had enjoyed before they were taken away seven months ago. It also included specific steps for reassigning some of the parts of Marlene's job that she couldn't do and that could be accomplished more productively by others in the department.
- The more that Albert and Marlene began to work together on redesigning her job assignments, the more motivated Marlene became for doing the hard work that was necessary to complete the project that was so important to Albert's future.

Instead of seeing a Space Case as someone who is consciously trying to undermine your interests at work, it helps to find out exactly why this individual feels unmotivated and resistant. Only when you know the real feelings of a Space Case can you begin to develop solutions that will help this person do a much better job.

I recommend the following steps for improving a frustrating situation with a Space Case:

- Either with a consultant or just the two of you, sit down and have a face-to-face brainstorming session on how to redesign a task so that it feels more interesting and motivating to the person.
- Find out what parts of the job this person enjoys and would like to handle more often.
- Find out what parts of the job tend to make this person feel bored, rebellious, or incompetent.

- Ask this person what she or he will need in order to feel more committed and involved in the job that needs to be done.
- Work together to discover ways to bring out the best in both of you. Even if the job can't be redesigned exactly the way both of you might like, see if you can motivate this person by becoming allies and working together toward goals you both find meaningful.

The Fourth Level: Describe Exactly What You Need and Let the Space Case Know What Your Limits Are

At the same time that you are seeking to understand what this Space Case needs in order to feel more motivated, make sure this person understands what your needs and limits are. Until you make your needs and limits explicitly clear, the Space Case will continue to do things that get on your nerves.

Most of us go through life trying to be self-reliant and not wanting to ask for too much from anyone. But there are certain situations, especially at work, that call for something different. These situations require that you verbalize your limitations and be clear with someone about exactly what you need or else he or she will continue to disappoint you.

What do I mean when I suggest you describe exactly what you need? I don't mean that you have to become a brutal or nasty tyrant. In fact, with most Space Cases, if you use an authoritarian style, it only makes them more spacey and distracted. Think about the Three Stooges for a moment. Moe was the angry, authoritarian brother who was forever trying to get the spacey brother, Curly, to be more focused and competent. Yet the more Moe yelled at Curly, the more Curly made mistakes or acted out in funny and inappropriate ways.

What works much more effectively with a Space Case is

to sit down with this person and spell out in clear-cut, specific details exactly what pressure you are under and what kind of help you need from this person. In other words, don't use fear or threats on a Space Case, who is likely to become even more distracted and rebellious in response. It is far more successful to elicit compassion and caring from a Space Case. This individual will often stop what he or she is doing to help you out if you ask for help.

Setting firm limits and asking for help from a Space Case essentially wakes this person up and makes him or her feel more responsible. It is far more effective than belittling this person.

For example, Raphael supervises a number of people at his job and has been battling for months with one particular employee who is a bit of a Space Case. His story illustrates how frustrating it can be to keep yelling at a Space Case, who only ignores your threats, and how effective it can be to sit down and ask for this person's help in a manner that makes the Space Case feel more involved.

Here's what Raphael told me during our initial consultation:

> For almost nine months I was acting like a tyrant to get this one guy in my department to do a better job. His name is Donald and he's intelligent but very easily distracted by just about anything except what he's supposed to be working on.
>
> So I would yell at Donald and threaten him with docking his pay. None of that worked. Donald would look at me with those faraway eyes of his and then he'd go right back to his flaky way of working.
>
> It didn't make any sense. I know that if I had a boss screaming at me and threatening to dock my pay, I'd shape up.

But as I advised Raphael, trying to become a conscientious person or shaping up is not the natural response of a Space Case. A spacey person has a different way of responding to threats or stressful situations. He or she gets distracted and foggy. Pure and simple. The more pressure you put on a Space Case, the more this person will get sidetracked by any interruptions or distractions that come along.

I advised Raphael to become more personal and vulnerable with Donald. If Raphael could stop yelling at Donald and begin asking him for help in a way that made Donald feel empowered and responsible, they might begin to have a better working relationship. Specifically, I urged Raphael to sit down and talk with Donald about three specific things:

1. Tell the spacey individual how much pressure you are under and how much you need this person to help you out. Instead of acting authoritarian and invincible, let this person know how vulnerable and at risk you are. Appeal to this person's sense of compassion and treat him or her as an adult rather than a child.

2. Spell out in specific detail exactly when you need this task completed and what negative consequences will happen to you or to your department if it's not done on time. Let the spacey individual know that a lot of people are depending on him or her to come through on this project.

3. Set up a close rapport with this individual so that you can make frequent checks on how the work is going. That means you will be calling this Space Case several times to see if the work has gotten started, to see if snags have delayed anything, to see if obstacles can be overcome, and to make sure it gets done on time.

What I told Raphael is what I advise anyone who is working with a Space Case: Since the spacey individual has trouble staying focused on a goal and can easily get interrupted or sidetracked, your job is to become the most important and heartfelt interruption that grabs this person's attention. Instead of feeling victimized that a Space Case gets interrupted easily, I recommend that you be the interruption. Every time you call this person up on the phone to make sure things are getting done on time, you become the most recent interruption. The Space Case will focus on helping you if he or she feels responsible for your welfare and if this person is reminded constantly of how important this is for you.

Once again, this works only if you spell out your needs to the Space Case and let him or her feel responsible for helping you out. It doesn't work if you treat the Space Case as an irresponsible, reprimanded child.

When Raphael took this advice and began to change the way he related to Donald, something interesting happened. According to Raphael:

> I never realized that what makes Donald such a spacey person is that he is frequently pushing aside his own projects and responding to the crises of everyone around him. Donald would be in the middle of an important project, but then he'd get sidetracked because a friend would call on the phone and start talking about a pressing personal issue. Or Donald would forget to work on his own projects because he'd get into a discussion with someone from another department who wanted his advice about how to handle her own work-related crisis. So I decided to stop being Donald's mean boss and become one of the people who needs his help and therefore can grab his attention.

Raphael took Donald out to lunch and told him about how much pressure he was under. He confided in Donald just how badly he needed this specific project to be done on time. Raphael even told Donald something he had never confided to another employee: "I'm dependent on you, Donald. You can make me or break me. Please don't let this project get pushed aside."

Here's what Raphael accomplished by changing the way he related to Donald:

For the first time in nine months, I actually got Donald's attention. He seemed genuinely concerned that his efforts could help me or hurt me professionally. For the first time that I can recall, I saw Donald much more motivated to work hard for me.

But that wasn't enough. Raphael still had to follow up. He had to keep repeating his needs and limits to Donald. Every other day, Raphael would see that Donald was getting distracted by someone else's cry for help or by some other interruption.

So Raphael took a few minutes each day, either on the phone or in person, to tell Donald once again just how worried he was about his project and how much was riding on Donald's results.

Raphael describes how

It wasn't easy keeping Donald focused on the project, but I didn't stop asking for my needs and he did get the job done. For once he was on time and his work was excellent. I didn't enjoy having to ask so many times for his help, but in the end it was worth it. He really came through.

If you find yourself working with a Space Case, you may need to be as persistent as Raphael was in handling Donald. You may need to sit down and have a heart-to-heart talk about how much your job or your company is on the line and how much you need this person's help. You may need to make several phone calls each week to find out how this person is progressing on your project. Don't assume the Space Case has changed miraculously into a conscientious worker. But do continue to treat this person with care and warmth. Remember that a Space Case gets spacier if you yell and act authoritarian, but this spacey person can become motivated and work harder if you say, ''Help! I need you!''

Here's one more example that illustrates how persistence

and personal rapport can improve your situation with a Space Case. Cheryl is the design manager in charge of an exciting new product for a large company. One of her most important suppliers, however, is a spacey person named Rudy who sometimes forgets to return phone calls and who often fails to meet crucial deadlines.

For several months, Cheryl was a bundle of nerves every time she had to rely on Rudy. She recalls,

> I would get so anxious knowing that I was at the mercy of this flaky person. If he messes up or gets too involved in someone else's project so that he forgets to return my calls or ship me the supplies I need, then I'm the one who's held responsible. It may be his incompetence, but it's my ass that's on the line. I remember feeling so powerless and complaining to Rudy each time he'd mess up, but the more I complained, the more he seemed to tune me out.

After Cheryl came to see me for several sessions during which she explored her frustrations about Rudy, she began experimenting with more creative ways of handling this Space Case. What worked for Cheryl? Here's her description:

> I had this enormously important assignment coming up and I knew I had to get a huge order from Rudy. I was terrified that he would mess up again and I'd be in a jam. But this time I got creative.
>
> First, I took Rudy out to lunch and really got to know him as an individual. I found out about the pressures he was under at work and with his family situation. I also let him know how much pressure I was under to meet certain deadlines and to make sure nothing went wrong with this important assignment. That established a rapport between us. I'm not saying I like this guy or that I'd trust him to babysit for my kids or even my dog. But I had built enough rapport

with him that I could feel good about calling him several times a week to chat briefly and find out how things were going on his end of this important project.

I'm sure he thought I was a little pushy. But my pushiness was mixed with enough personal warmth to make these phone calls enjoyable. Almost every day, I brainstormed with him to help him overcome each of the roadblocks that could have made him late on this project. Treating Rudy like an important ally got the job done! And it was a lot more pleasant than in the past when I sat back and let him ignore me and put everyone else's needs first.

As Cheryl discovered, breaking through Rudy's spaciness was worth the effort. Not only did she prevent another missed deadline, but she no longer felt powerless or victimized by Rudy's spacey habits. According to Cheryl,

Rudy is still a Space Case. I didn't change that. But I did find a way to get him to keep his promises and meet the deadlines that were important to me and my assignment. That was what I needed and from now on I know how to keep him from causing me problems.

7

Don't Let an Invalidator Ruin Your Day

A few years ago, my wife Linda and I hiked down the South Rim of the Grand Canyon to begin a nine day white-water rafting trip along the Colorado River.

While we were hiking the steep mountain trail, which has dozens of abrupt hairpin turns as it descends almost eleven miles to the river, we kept running into a father and his three children who were hiking along the same canyon trail.

From a distance, it looked as though the father was teaching his kids about the Grand Canyon. He seemed to be talking to them constantly.

But as we got within fifty yards of the man, we could hear that he was relentlessly picking at his kids and criticizing them for doing things wrong on the trail.

The first time we passed this father and his three children, we heard him snapping at his younger son to stop swinging his arms when he walked.

"Keep your arms close to your sides," the father instructed.

"Why?" the younger son asked.

"Because I say so," the father insisted.

The next time we happened to be walking near this

131

family, we heard the father chastising the daughter for walking too slowly.

"I'm just looking at the scenery," she said.

"We never should have brought you along," the father replied.

"But I like slowing down to look," she argued.

"You're ruining it for everyone," the father said.

Later we passed this troubled family again at a covered rest stop on the trail where we heard him picking at the eldest son for not using the compass correctly.

The father said to his son, "Don't you know how to use that thing?"

"Yes, I can use it," the son replied.

"No you can't. You're holding it wrong. Let me show you."

"You already showed me, Dad. Give me a chance." The son's voice sounded as though tears were beginning to well up in his eyes.

"Give me that," the father insisted. "You don't know what you're doing."

As the father grabbed the compass from the eldest son, we could see the boy's face tense up with embarrassment and anger.

I've thought about that troubled family at the Grand Canyon many times since that afternoon. What was it like for these three kids living with their hypercritical father day after day after day? How do you survive when someone is breathing down your neck and finding fault with everything you do?

The Frustration of Working with an Invalidator

Quite often as a therapist, I hear work-related stories from people that sound similar to the story of the troubled family hiking in the Grand Canyon. Many of us work with someone who is extremely negative and nitpicking. It might be a particular boss, coworker, business partner, or customer who never seems satisfied. Perhaps you work with a perfectionist who relentlessly finds fault. Or it could be an insecure colleague who criticizes your work to make you feel small so that he or she can feel big.

Sooner or later, all of us encounter at work an Invalidator—someone who is less explosive than an Angry Screamer, but who nonetheless is excessively picky and dissatisfied. An Invalidator usually doesn't scream or shout; instead, this person whines, complains, criticizes, and makes everyone else insecure.

How do you respond to that kind of person? How do you keep your sense of self-confidence and professionalism when you are faced with someone who second-guesses your every decision or who seems to take pride in making you wrong?

Stop for a moment and think about an Invalidator that you currently have to deal with. Is there someone in your work life who tends to find fault with almost everything you do? What is it about this person's way of talking to you that feels so negative and nitpicking? Is it the tone of voice this person uses when giving criticism? Is it the picky complaints this person bombards you with that make you feel lousy after every conversation? Is it an attitude this person sends off that is so irritating? Or is it simply the quantity of negative remarks he or she makes?

What Can Be Done?

This chapter is about how to deal more successfully with someone whose fault finding is hard to take. How do you stop this person from undermining your own sense of competence? How do you make sure an Invalidator doesn't ruin your projects or your peace of mind?

Step #1: Find Out Exactly Why This Invalidator Is So Negative

If you would like to improve your situation with someone at work who frequently is nitpicking or critical, it's essential that you begin to uncover why this person acts this way. The more you understand what makes an Invalidator tick, the easier it will be to stand up to this person and not get destroyed by his or her negativity. Take a look at the following four characteristics of the typical Invalidator. See how many of them apply to the boss, coworker, or customer who is giving you a hard time at work.

The Invalidator Thinks It's His or Her Duty to Find Something Wrong: It might not be written formally in this person's job description, but somewhere in this person's mind there is a duty, an obligation, a reason for living that he or she must find something wrong with everything you say or do.

Sometimes it takes some probing before the Invalidator finds out exactly what can be criticized about the task you've performed, but if there is a flaw or a questionable issue to be discovered, this individual will spot it.

Why does an Invalidator feel so compelled to find mistakes? It might be that this person once had a mentor or a boss who was extremely critical and demanding. So the Invalidator decided that to sound intelligent one must be as picky as that previous role model.

Or the Invalidator might have grown up with an extremely critical father or mother who had the most power in the family. So the Invalidator grew up thinking subconsciously, "When I'm an adult and I have some say-so in the work world, I'm going to be tough and critical like the parent who made me squirm all those times."

Or the Invalidator might have had some bad experiences when he or she wasn't sufficiently nitpicking or critical. Possibly a mistake slipped past this person's attention and it caused a serious problem. Maybe this individual was humiliated and lost a job or a business because of being too tolerant of other people's mistakes. So the Invalidator made a conscious vow or an unconscious decision to be sure a similar kind of thing never happened again. ''From now on,'' this person might have decided, ''I'm going to keep looking at each detail to find something that might be incorrect and then I'll never get burned again.''

Whatever the original motivation for this Invalidator to be so finicky and unpleasant, the fact remains that this person cannot rest or relax until some probing uncovers something for which this individual can find fault. Even it you do an excellent job with an Invalidator, this person still needs to find something to complain about or worry about. It's as essential to this person as breathing is to the rest of us.

The Invalidator Has a Tone of Voice or a Way of Speaking that Is Hard to Take: When an Invalidator picks apart your work or criticizes you for the hundredth time, it is not just the words that this person uses but also the tone of voice or way of speaking that can be irritating.

For example, some Invalidators have a whiny tone that could make a dog howl. You work real hard on something and then you show it to an Invalidator. You're hoping for some acknowledgment or some encouragement. Instead, you get this whiny, negative complaining that not only criticizes the work you've done but also grates on your nerves like nails on a blackboard.

Other Invalidators have a flat, monotone way of criticizing people that includes clenching his or her teeth and not opening the jaw. You're looking at this individual talking to you and you see that his or her face is tensed up in an embittered snarl. The critical words are spoken out of the sides of this person's mouth. It's as though he or she feels that what you've done is so disgusting it doesn't warrant opening the mouth and talking freely about it.

Still other Invalidators have a staccato way of snapping at

you in short bursts of interrogative questioning or harsh disapproval. The words jump out at you like quick slaps that startle your senses and feel like a hostile barrage. The rapid-fire questioning makes you feel defensive. The quick bursts of disapproval feel like a personal attack.

When you think about the highly critical individual you work with, what exactly about this person's way of speaking do you find the most irritating? Stop and notice the next time you are with this person. Is it the whininess? Is it the short staccato bursts of disapproval? Is it the way this person grits his or her teeth while speaking? Is it the way this person glances at you with condescension or distrust? Or is it some other specific behavior that lets you know you are being singled out for criticism?

To an Invalidator, Life Is a Constant Battle to Appear Right and in Control: It's not easy for an Invalidator to admit that someone else might also be right, or that some other point of view might be equally valid.

In a conversation with an Invalidator you might have thought the goal was working together toward a common solution to a problem that affects both of you at work. But in most cases, the Invalidator has a very different goal than that. In almost every conversation at work, an Invalidator seeks to use whatever details he or she can come up with to prove two things: (1) that the Invalidator is in control, and (2) that someone else is to blame.

It can be extremely frustrating for you to be confronted repeatedly by this person who is trying to prove his or her rightness, even in situations where it doesn't matter who's right or wrong. In addition, an Invalidator will tend to twist facts and information around to prove that he or she is right even when this person is clearly uninformed or incorrect.

For example, Boyd, a middle manager for a large firm, often feels frustrated when dealing with his immediate supervisor, Karl, who has many of the characteristics of an Invalidator. According to Boyd,

It's such a drain on my energy to have to discuss any problems or issues with Karl. I go into the conversation hoping we can work together to come up with a simple solution, but immediately Karl starts bombarding me with questions. Not questions about how to improve the situation, but questions about whose fault it is, who's to blame, or what went wrong. It starts feeling like an interrogation, as though I'm on trial for messing up. But all I was looking for is some input on how to resolve the problem without wasting a lot of time on who did what and who ought to be called on the carpet and reprimanded.

What Boyd experiences with Karl is what most people encounter when dealing with an Invalidator. The Invalidator is usually more concerned about defending his or her position and finding a way to criticize or blame others than in simply sitting down to brainstorm about a solution to the immediate problem. To an Invalidator, the important issue is not how to work together to improve things but who messed up, what they did wrong, why people are getting away with things, and who he or she can blame.

The Invalidator Lives in a Constant State of Worry and Dissatisfaction, Which Feels Normal to This Person: Quite often I counsel people who say they wish they could get an Invalidator to say to them, "Nice job," "You did good," or "You've done enough—way to go." What they don't realize is that an Invalidator sees the world differently and feels much more drawn to what's going wrong than to what's going right.

If you fill up a glass of water halfway and show it to an Invalidator, not only will this person say the glass is half empty, but he or she will also notice the spots, the imperfect way the glass is constructed, and the fingerprints on the outside of the glass. To an Invalidator, that isn't being overly critical, it's just the way this person sees the world.

For an Invalidator, worrying about what might go wrong

or feeling dissatisfied with whatever is going on is a normal state of affairs. The world is filled with people and things that don't live up to his or her expectations. Every day is another chance to be disappointed and to let people know how disappointed this person feels.

So the Invalidator you work with is not just unhappy with you or the work you do. This person finds fault with everyone he or she meets. If there were a Catholic church named after this kind of critical individual, it would be Our Lady of Perpetual Dissatisfaction.

If your goal is to please an Invalidator or make this person finally feel satisfied, good luck! The very essence of being an Invalidator means that this person is almost never satisfied nor thinks something is good enough. To live inside an Invalidator's mind is to constantly worry that some minor detail is going to wreck everything. What a way to live!

Step #2: Use Your Sense of Humor to Take the Sting Out of This Person's Critical Remarks

Now that you recognize some of the specific characteristics of the Invalidator, how do you deal more effectively with this kind of critical individual? How do you make sure this person's picking at you doesn't wipe you out?

If an Invalidator clobbers you with criticism and it causes you to lose your sense of who you are and what you're good at, then the Invalidator has been victorious. You have been reduced to mush.

To prevent this from happening to you, I recommend having at your disposal a very quick and simple technique that allows you to take the sting out of this person's critical remarks immediately as they are occurring.

A humorous technique I have seen work wonders for many women and men who are dealing with an Invalidator goes like this: As soon as the Invalidator starts to ask probing, fault-finding questions or begins to make critical remarks, take a deep breath in and out as you humorously say to yourself, "Thank goodness! My life would not be complete without this person's criticism." Silently and with a touch of sarcastic irony, have a good private laugh as you listen to this person picking at your work and as you block his or her negativity by saying to yourself in a cheerful tone, "Thank goodness! My life would not be complete without this person's criticism."

Just one simple statement to protect your psyche and help you remain strong and alert.

Don't say it out loud! But do say it several times to yourself as you are being bombarded by this critical individual. Even if it sounds strange, say it to yourself anyway.

Why does this work? Why does saying, "Thank goodness! My life would not be complete without this person's criticism" take the sting out of potentially invalidating remarks? There are several reasons why this simple act of using a silent bit of sarcasm does the trick for most women and men who try it.

- Using your own wit and sarcasm in a safe and unspoken way gives you a feeling of protective distance that the Invalidator can't take away from you.
- Having a sense of humor when you're under fire tells your emotions and your biochemistry not to panic. It says, "Don't worry. We're gonna be all right. No need to launch the old fight-or-flight hormones. This is just a drill and not a real emergency."
- Most importantly, when you sound smart and in control to yourself, it allows you to remain smart and in control over your eventual response to this Invalidator. Instead of feeling like a scolded child, you can remain an intelligent and competent adult in this important work situation.

Here's an example of someone who used this humor technique to change the way she reacted to an extremely critical Invalidator.

Devra is a thirty-two-year-old woman who runs a research department for a consulting firm. She usually feels competent and professional at her job, except when she has to deal with a certain fault-finding and critical woman named Georgianne. When Devra gets bombarded by Georgianne's invalidating remarks, Devra often forgets she is thirty-two and competent. Instead, she tends to feel around twelve years old and very unsure of herself.

According to Devra:

> Georgianne knows exactly how to take whatever I've done and make it seem worthless. She picks apart my methodology until I lose my confidence in my own decisions. She finds a way to say, "But you forgot to consider this," or "I'm surprised you didn't think of doing that."
>
> There has never been a project I've done with Georgianne where she didn't make me feel incompetent. She is so nitpicking and critical, I dread having to call her on the phone or meet with her in person.

When Devra came to see me in my office, she was thinking about quitting her job. But after several years of working her way up to become the head of the research department, it didn't seem fair to either of us that she would have to leave the company because of how unpleasant it is to work with Georgianne.

So I recommended to Devra that she begin changing the way she reacts to Georgianne. The first step would be to use this humor technique to take the sting out of Georgianne's critical remarks. At first, Devra was hesitant. She told me:

> Why should I sit there and say, "Thank goodness! My life would not be complete without Georgianne's criticism"? It sounds so passive and it almost encourages Georgianne to keep treating me in a condescending way.

As I explained to Devra, the reason for using this humor technique as a first step toward becoming more effective with an Invalidator is not to make you more passive or compliant. Rather, it is to use your silent sarcasm to keep you feeling strong and adult rather than letting your emotions fall back into the rut of feeling like a scolded child.

Devra still wasn't sure it would work—that is, until she tried it out in a tense situation with Georgianne. Here's what happened.

Devra had worked late into the night on a Thursday evening to complete an important research project that she had to show to Georgianne on Friday morning. When Georgianne began looking at the information, immediately there were nitpicking questions and a harshly critical tone of voice. "Why didn't you think about doing it this way?" "I'm worried about whether we've left out too much of the earlier draft." "I think you ought to work on this some more."

As often happens, Devra began to feel scolded, belittled, and powerless in response to Georgianne's negativity. But this time Devra tried out the humor technique and began saying repeatedly to herself, "Thank goodness! My life would not be complete without Georgianne's criticism."

To her surprise, Devra noticed some immediate changes. She recalls:

It was very interesting. Instead of feeling foggy and shut down because Georgianne was criticizing my work, I kept repeating silently the sarcastic lines, and I actually felt much stronger and more adult.

Because I didn't shut down this time, I found it much easier to remain in control and to explain to Georgianne the logic behind each of my decisions. She got me to rewrite a few of the paragraphs in my report, but overall I was extremely successful in getting Georgianne to see that some of her fears and criticisms were unnecessary.

Having the ability to laugh silently to myself at

Georgianne's excessive pickiness and to pretend that my life would not be complete without her criticism has made me a lot less passive and a lot more articulate in standing up for my point of view.

The next time you are being criticized by an Invalidator at work, don't just take it into your emotional system without first taking the sting out of the remarks. Use your sense of humor. Keep your sense of perspective and self-confidence. Silently laugh to yourself as you say, "Thank goodness! My life would not be complete without this person's criticism."

Step #3: Whenever Possible, Get a Second Opinion Rather Than Accepting an Invalidator's Subjective Criticism as the Ultimate Truth

When an Invalidator picks apart your work or questions your worthiness, it's quite tempting to believe this person is the final word on the subject. There's something about the way an Invalidator says, "I'm right and you better believe I'm right" that makes even the most self-confident people start to question their own value.

We all have someone in our lives who knows exactly how to make us feel small, incompetent, or unworthy. Even if you say to yourself, "This time I'm not going to let that person get to me," the Invalidator is relentless in picking at your work or finding a problem in even the most terrific results. You will need more than good intentions to change the way you respond to someone who is a master at making others feel unsure of themselves. You will need to improve your way of sorting out what is useful and what is unnecessarily invalidating about this person's remarks to you.

The specific step I recommend to people for handling a nitpicking person is to make sure you get a reliable second opinion to assess the Invalidator's criticisms and to identify:

- Which part of the feedback is accurate and which part of the feedback is just this person's negative way of complaining about everything?
- What part of the feedback is useful to your work, and what part is incorrect, misinformed, or just plain whiny?
- Which one of the fears or concerns of the Invalidator needs to be investigated, and which of these worries are a waste of your time and energy?

If you have a boss, coworker, or customer who tends to be an Invalidator, then you will need to have some quickly accessible sources for getting a reliable second opinion to verify or discard the problems raised by the Invalidator. Otherwise, you will be constantly fluctuating between two dangerous extremes: (1) to blindly accept the Invalidator's feedback as the final word on the subject, or (2) to blindly rebel against the Invalidator's comments, even if they are sometimes accurate and useful.

Most people get agitated when they are criticized by an Invalidator. As a result, they either blindly accept the criticism they receive from this person, hoping it will shut the person up, or they blindly rebel against even the most potentially useful feedback if it comes out of the mouth of a highly critical Invalidator. Both of these extremes are dangerous because you are reacting with incomplete information. You are accepting harsh criticism that might be baloney, or you are rejecting possibly excellent feedback that happens to have been delivered by a negative person.

Where can you get a good second opinion to help you sort out the criticism you receive from an Invalidator? Here are some possible sources for quick and useful second opinions. See which of the following are available to you now or could become available if you make sure to seek out these kinds of individuals:

- Is there a good friend or respected ally at work who could help you sort out which part of the Invalidator's criticism is useful and which part is to be ignored?

- Is there someone in your profession or industry that you could call in a crisis who would give you reliable information about the accuracy of this Invalidator's comments and suggestions?
- Is there someone you can call or visit who has a great deal of expertise on the specific issues criticized by the Invalidator and who could help you decide what is fact and what is opinion?
- Do you have a close friend, family member, counselor, or therapist who can help you regain your sense of self-confidence and professionalism even when you have just been picked at by an Invalidator?

When you call or visit one of these individuals to get a second opinion on something that an Invalidator has criticized, make sure you identify what the situation is and exactly what you are looking for. Here are some examples that will illustrate how to go about getting a second opinion to help you sort out the criticism from an Invalidator:

Calling an Expert You Don't Know Personally: You might introduce yourself and say you need a quick bit of expertise from this person who was recommended to you by someone you know in common. Then ask this expert, ''I just spoke with someone who said —————— is true. Based on your best information, how would you evaluate the situation and what would you say in response to that person?''

Calling Someone You Know Personally Who Happens to Be an Expert on the Topic: Let this person know exactly what's going on—that you have a very critical person you're dealing with at work who disagrees with you on a specific issue. Then ask this individual, ''If you were in my shoes, what would you find useful in that person's criticisms and what would you tend to ignore?''

Asking for Emotional Support from a Friend, Family Member, Counselor, or Therapist: As soon as possible after an Invalidator has belittled you or your work, call this supportive individual and explain, ''I just got out of a meeting where I had a bomb dropped on my head by —————————. Would you please remind me that I do have the qualifications to be doing this work, and that I am an adult, and that I do deserve to hold my head up even though ————————— thinks I'm an idiot?''

Don't be afraid to ask for support. Whether you are looking for a second opinion that informs you about a specific piece of factual information or whether you are looking for an emotional boost so that you don't get shut down by an Invalidator's criticisms, be sure to make the phone call and get the support you need. People usually like to be asked for their expertise and their guidance. If the person you call is too busy at that moment to listen to your situation, find a more convenient time or else call another person who can give you the information or guidance you require.

Sandra's case illustrates how important it is to ask for both informational support and emotional support after you've gotten clobbered by an extremely critical Invalidator.

Sandra is the owner of a small computer software firm and she frequently has to deal with customers and suppliers who are Invalidators. According to Sandra,

One of my most important customers is a guy named Terence, who is the computer systems manager for a large firm. Terence is a real techno-nerd who always has to be right. He talks to me like I'm a complete idiot and he's always trying to prove that he's more up to date and informed than anyone else about what's happening in computer software.

I often feel drained and exhausted when I have to deal with Terence about a problem in our software or a new project at his company where they might need our help. He's so relentless in his negative remarks and his ''I'm right and you're wrong'' attitude. But I can't tell him to go to hell because his company is one of my best accounts.

When Sandra came to my office for advice on how to handle Terence and several other difficult people she works with, I explained to her about the importance of getting a reliable second opinion with both up-to-date information and emotional support whenever she was getting picked at by an Invalidator like Terence. I told her, "Even if you know your facts perfectly, an Invalidator can still pick at you until you lose your self-confidence. That's why you need to have quick phone access to one or two people who can remind you that you do know what you're talking about and that you don't deserve this kind of treatment."

Sandra immediately saw the benefit of getting a fact-oriented second opinion if Terence tried to put her down and compete over who was more up to date on technical information. Sandra commented, "There are two colleagues I can call for technical advice whenever Terence tries to make me feel stupid. These two people are unbeatable when it comes to knowing the latest information, and they'll tell me what I need to know to stand up to Terence's arguments and to see what part of Terence's information is worth taking seriously."

But like many people in work situations, Sandra was reluctant to ask anyone for emotional support. She told me, "What is the point? Terence is a jerk. I don't let him get to me. I don't need emotional support."

Yet for the past several months, Sandra had been working on a difficult project with Terence's company and she had been experiencing not only a mild depression but also some physical symptoms from the stresses of dealing on a daily basis with an extremely toxic person. Sandra had been having painful headaches and later discovered that a minor skin rash had flared up into a serious infection on her arms and back. While we were discussing these problems, Sandra explained,

I don't know for certain if I've been having these headaches and skin flare-ups because of Terence and the whole mess at his company. I've been stressed out lately for a variety of reasons. But I do know that there's something about working with Terence that lowers my resistance to these physical and emotional problems. Especially when I'm tired or overworked, Terence knows exactly how to pick at me and get me to feel unsure of myself because of how adamant he is about his opinions. He somehow knows how to wear me down and make me lose my self-confidence. I wind up giving in and letting him control the project. As soon as that happens, my moods and my physical problems get even worse.

I asked Sandra if she was willing to try an experiment. Would she be willing to call one or two of her closest friends and ask for emotional support immediately before and after her encounters with Terence, just to see if it made a difference? Sandra said she'd give it a try.

For the next few weeks, Sandra started a new habit of calling one of her close friends for a quick emotional boost before and after her face-to-face meetings with Terence. She asked her friend, "Can you remind me during these phone calls that I am intelligent and strong, even if Terence tries to make me feel stupid and weak?"

This phone support came in handy a few days later when a major foul-up occurred in a computer system Sandra was developing for Terence's company. Terence blamed the entire mess on Sandra. Even though she knew she was not the primary source of the problem, Sandra did feel a certain sense of guilt and responsibility. She recalls:

I felt so frustrated and lousy about the whole thing. I worried that I might lose the entire account. I kept wondering if somehow the foul-up had been my fault, even though I knew it wasn't because of my doing anything wrong. I couldn't focus on any of my other projects. This mess at Terence's company was on my mind almost the entire day and it even started keeping me up at night.

So I called not only my technical advisors but also one of my friends for emotional support before my next meeting with Terence. I asked my friend, "Please remind me. Do I have the brains and the persistence to handle situations like this? Am I going to let this creep throw me off my rhythm or am I going to make sure this account gets my best effort to resolve the problem?"

My friend gave me exactly the pep talk I needed. I got off the phone remembering again that I do have the ability to handle situations like this. It would take time to resolve the mess, but now I had my self-confidence back and I could focus clearly on some possible solutions.

I called Terence back and set up a problem-solving meeting. No more fault finding or blaming anyone. From then on, I took charge and got people thinking about solutions. It took several weeks to fix the situation, but I did get the job done. I didn't lose that account, and more importantly, I found out that I can keep my sanity and be strong with someone as difficult as Terence.

Like Sandra, each of us needs not only technical support but also emotional support when we're bombarded by the belittling remarks of an Invalidator. If someone is constantly picking at your work and undermining your self-confidence, now might be a good time to begin getting the reliable second opinions and support you need.

Step #4: Teach This Invalidator How You Want to Be Treated

Since an Invalidator automatically focuses on what's going wrong and has trouble noticing anything that's going right, you will need to actively teach this person how to treat you in a more tolerable fashion. Rather than waiting for an Invalidator to miraculously change into a less critical person, there are specific things you can do to improve the way this person treats you, even if he or she doesn't change his or her basic personality.

I recommend to those who want to be treated better by an extremely critical or negative person that you turn the issue of feedback and criticism into a game that is played by a few simple rules that you will need to teach the person you work with:

Rule #1: Tell the Critical Individual That You Want to Hear What's Wrong, But Only After You've Been Told at Least Three Things That Have Been Done Right: You can say to this person, "I do want to hear what can be improved, but first we need to find at least three things that are in good shape right now."

This might not be easy for an Invalidator to do. He or she might start picking at or finding fault with even those things that are perfectly fine. But you must stick to the rules of the game and keep repeating to this individual, "I do want to hear what can be improved, but first we need to find at least three things that are in good shape right now."

For example, Glenda tried out this first rule on her coworker Sharlene, who is an extremely nitpicking and critical individual. According to Glenda, "Every time I work on a project with Sharlene, all she does is find fault. I never hear anything but criticism and complaints from Sharlene."

To begin improving the way Sharlene and Glenda work together on projects, Glenda suggested, "Let's try something new. In a few minutes we'll get a chance to make suggestions on what can be improved about this project. But first let's try something different. Is it possible to find three things that are good or even excellent before we start finding things wrong?"

Glenda recalls that Sharlene didn't think too highly of this suggestion. Sharlene commented, "What's the point in

finding things that are fine when there's so much that needs
to be fixed?''

Without giving in, Glenda repeated the first rule and said,
''I do want to hear what can be improved, but first we need
to find at least three things that are in good shape right
now.''

Sharlene thought the exercise was silly, but she went
along with it at Glenda's insistence. And for the first time in
their working relationship, Glenda and Sharlene began to
work as a team. First they both took turns describing three
things they each liked about the project thus far. Then they
both took turns describing those things they would want to
fix or improve.

Glenda discovered that ''It's so much easier to listen to
Sharlene's critical remarks after I've heard some positive
feedback from her. It was so much more balanced and less
of an attack.''

When you insist that an Invalidator tell you three things
that are all right before letting this person tell you what's not
right, you accomplish two important goals:

1. You are teaching this person that if he or she wants
   to criticize something about your work, there first has
   to be some acknowledgment of what's good about
   your work.

2. You are making sure that this person doesn't just
   start attacking your work, which can make you feel
   defensive or frustrated. Instead, you teach this person
   how to give a more balanced and realistic feedback
   of pluses and minuses that are easier to hear than
   minuses alone.

**Rule #2: Don't Wait for This Person to Bombard You
with Global, Generalized, Negative Comments—Take
Charge and Ask for Specific, Useful, Constructive Ideas:**
Once you have insisted that the Invalidator give you three
things that are going right before giving you negative

feedback, then it's time to take charge of a second aspect of the game of criticism.

Instead of letting the Invalidator make you feel small because he or she gives out global, generalized, negative comments, you can feel strong and competent by actively directing your own questions at this person. Rather than holding your breath and dreading that the Invalidator will criticize you, take charge and ask questions to make sure the criticism you receive is specific, useful, and constructive.

Be direct and ask this overly critical person for two specific things: First, don't settle for a vague or general critique such as "This is no good" or "I don't like it," but instead ask for a specific and useful critique, such as, "Exactly what part did you feel could be improved?" Second, don't wait for an Invalidator to volunteer constructive new ideas, but rather seek out his or her ideas by asking, "What would you like this part to be like?"

For example, Tony is a film editor who recently was brought in to work on a project that is being supervised by a producer named Corbin. According to Tony,

> Corbin is a nightmare to work with. He's so negative and so unspecific. He'll look at my work and frown. Then he'll lean back and with total self-assuredness say, "This is no good. It doesn't work. It simply doesn't work."
>
> That's as specific as Corbin gets. It's like he's a medieval lord and you get called into his inner chamber and he leans back and says, "This is no good. Off with his head."

When Tony asked me for suggestions on how to deal with producers like Corbin who are extremely negative and not very helpful, I gave him the following guidelines for taking charge of conversations with an Invalidator and making sure the criticism he receives is specific, useful, and constructive:

- Start by asking the critical person for a specific moment when he or she started to feel the work wasn't right. You might need to read or restate the specific words or images to help this person recall exactly when it started to feel wrong. You need the exact moment that can be fixed.

- Then ask the critical person what he or she was looking for at that moment and didn't receive. What was this person hoping to hear or see? What was this person anticipating might happen and what would have felt a lot better to this person if it had happened? Even if the Invalidator isn't good at giving positive suggestions, most people can still recall what they were hoping for and wanted to see happen. Your job is to find out exactly what this individual was hoping for at a specific part of your project and then see if you can use that feedback to improve your project.

Tony put these two guidelines into practice during his next meeting with the producer Corbin. Corbin had looked over Tony's daily edits and made one of his usual global criticisms, saying, "Oh my God! This is terrible. This will never work."

Following my instructions, Tony took charge and made sure to find out exactly at what moment in the project Corbin had begun to feel disappointed.

At first Corbin resisted his efforts to make the criticism less global and more specific. Corbin groaned, "There's no point in focusing on one specific moment. The whole thing stinks. It's all got to be changed."

But Tony stayed in control of the situation and kept asking Corbin, "Was it here? What about here? What about this specific moment?" After a few minutes of probing by Tony, Corbin did recall the exact moment when his interest and expectations turned into frustration and disappointment.

Now Tony had some useful feedback from the producer. There was a specific moment in the project when Corbin had become disappointed. The criticism was no longer global and unspecific. Tony knew the exact spot where the troubles began and could be fixed.

The next step was for Tony to ask Corbin exactly what the producer was hoping for and anticipating at that specific moment. This, too, took some probing by Tony before Corbin finally recalled that he had been hoping for something specific that didn't happen, and as a result he felt disappointed. Now Tony not only knew the exact moment that needed repair but also had some possible ideas from Corbin about what might work.

Taking an active role and making sure you get the most specific and useful information out of an Invalidator is no easy task. It might take patience and persistence before you succeed in turning the global put-downs by an Invalidator into helpful and valuable feedback. But it's clearly worth the effort if you can find out exactly what caused the Invalidator to turn sour on your work and what might cause a less negative reaction. Unless you take charge and insist on specific feedback, you will be left with nothing but useless put-downs.

Step #5: Instead of Remaining Victimized by an Invalidator, Begin to See This Person as an Opportunity to Come to Terms With Your Own Inner Critic

Now we come to the final step for changing the way you respond to an extremely critical individual at work. Instead of paying attention to what the Invalidator is doing, however, in this final step your task is to pay attention to what goes on inside your own mind in terms of self-criticism and internalized negative feedback.

Rather than pretending that all the criticism is coming from someone outside of you, now it's time to face the fact that the most painful criticism at work might be coming from inside your own Inner Critic. Most human beings spend a good portion of every working day bombarding themselves with unrealistically high expectations, harsh criticisms, and angry put-downs of the things you don't do well. Is it any wonder you feel defensive and frustrated when an Invalidator picks at your work or says out loud some of the harsh things your Inner Critic has said silently?

To improve the way you handle the Invalidator you work with as well as the Inner Critic you carry inside your mind, here are some crucial questions to ask yourself:

- When you make an error or an oversight at work, do you criticize yourself in a harsh manner?
- Before you show up for an important meeting, job interview, or work assignment, do your thoughts tend to stick with what you are afraid might go wrong or do you know how to envision ways of making things go right?
- When you are running late on a deadline, do you bombard yourself with anxious thoughts that you are going to be in big trouble—long before anyone outside of you has even noticed or commented that you're running late?
- Do you sometimes worry that you are going to be found out and that people are going to discover that you're not really able to do what's expected of you?
- Do you sometimes lie awake at night criticizing yourself for something that went wrong that day, even though you didn't have much or any control over what happened?
- Have you ever said or thought to yourself that you are your own worst critic?

If you have been putting up with your Inner Critic for many years and letting it bombard you with anxiety and negative feedback, now that you are also working with an Invalidator who is attacking you with criticism from outside might mean that all this criticism has gone too far. Something has got to change! Your emotional and physical well-being cannot continue to let the Inner Critic and the external Invalidator continue to drag your psyche through the mud.

What can be done to lessen the amount of self-criticism you experience at work? What can be done to reduce the harshness of your own Inner Critic?

In my work as a therapist and seminar leader, I have seen repeatedly that even the most intelligent and competent people are plagued by harsh Inner Critics. To be able to handle someone you work with who is an Invalidator, you will need to lessen the amount and severity of the criticism you heap on yourself. Some ways of doing that are:

Catch yourself immediately when you start to invalidate your own hard work and good intentions on a project that has setbacks or problems. Rather than attacking yourself with criticism, take a moment to stop and catch yourself. Ask yourself, "Is this self-criticism necessary or useful? Would my energy be better spent getting support and ideas for solutions?"

Instead of losing sight of all the good work you've done just because something has gone wrong, ask yourself, "Do I really need to invalidate all that I've done right on this project just because something has gone wrong? Could I address the problem from a stronger sense of professionalism if I keep in mind that I've done a lot of good work leading up to this crossroads?"

Remind yourself each day or evening of three good things you did that day. Most people remember only the things that go wrong and they focus only on the things that they can't fix or control.

Don't do that to yourself! At least once a day or at night when you are unwinding from work, take a few moments to acknowledge to yourself (or with someone you care about) the hard work and worthwhile efforts you did that day. Even if the project isn't done or if it hasn't turned out exactly as you planned, take stock of the valuable planning, thinking, and actions that you've taken that day or that week.

If you want to feel less victimized by someone you work with who is an Invalidator, then you need to start validating your own good work!

Use your frustrations at the way an Invalidator talks to you as a stimulus to make sure you don't talk to yourself in a similar manner. If you notice yourself saying or doing some of the mean things you can't stand about an Invalidator, make sure to stop yourself and say, "I don't need to be this mean to myself or anyone else."

In essence, an Invalidator can become your mentor or guru to teach you exactly what you don't want to be like. The more you notice how lousy it feels to be treated with harsh criticism and accusatory questions, the more you might want to avoid doing the same things to yourself and those people in your life who are important to you—your friends, your loved ones, your children, your coworkers, and especially yourself.

If you need extra help to stop being mistreated by an Invalidator or to stop being so critical with yourself, don't hesitate to ask for professional advice. The longer you wait, the more you will suffer physical or emotional problems if you have to keep listening to the harsh criticisms of an Invalidator or of your Inner Critic. Many women and men have made tremendous progress from discussing their difficulties about criticism with a helpful therapist or counselor. Your work, your success, your relationships, and your health will improve if you find a way to deal more effectively with the external criticism that will always be a part of any work environment.

Even if you quit your job or run away from a particular Invalidating person, sooner or later you will face a similar problem with criticism from either another Invalidator or from your own Inner Critic. That's why your best bet is to start today to seek professional help to learn how to handle criticism in a much better way.

• • •

When I think about someone who made tremendous progress in dealing with her own Inner Critic, I recall a therapy client named Marjorie. Because Marjorie grew up with two parents who were very critical perfectionists, any stressful situation at work could easily retrigger some painful emotions for her. If someone at work criticized Marjorie, it was hard for her to take it in and not feel defensive or hurt. In addition, Marjorie was so critical and perfectionistic herself, she rarely had a moment's peace when she wasn't second-guessing her own work.

Over a period of several months in therapy, Marjorie gained a lot of insights about why she had become so painfully self-critical and why it was so hard for her to handle others who were perfectionistic and invalidating. In addition to those insights, something happened during one of our therapy sessions that proved to be a turning point in the way Marjorie dealt with criticism and critical people.

One afternoon Marjorie came in for her weekly session and she seemed extremely anxious. That day at work she had made an innocent mistake that could cost her company thousands of dollars. Marjorie told me, "I'm so upset inside. This feels like a disaster for me. Someone is going to point a finger at me and say, 'See, I knew all along she doesn't know what she's doing.' I'm probably going to be fired for this, and my references for future jobs will be all ruined."

During that therapy session, Marjorie and I role-played what people at work might be saying about Marjorie's mistake. We also enacted what her mother would say and what her father would say. Finally, we did some creative role-playing about what Marjorie's Inner Critic might say.

This role-playing exercise was a chance for Marjorie to take charge of the fears and voices that had plagued her for years. With each character she enacted (the people at work, her mother, her father, her Inner Critic), Marjorie's energy and clarity of mind became much more calm and focused.

By the end of that therapy session, Marjorie felt different

inside—a lot less self-critical and a lot less fearful of the criticism of others. She had found during the role-playing exercise that the critical voices inside her mind were more manageable and less terrifying than she had previously felt. Like many therapy clients who have gotten stronger as a result of role-playing their fears and Inner Critics like this, Marjorie no longer felt like a passive victim of these internal voices.

Feeling more in charge of herself, Marjorie went to work the next day and took the initiative to begin cleaning up the mess that was created by her earlier mistake. She told me a few weeks later:

> My old reaction would have been to feel guilty and close down out of fear that someone would judge me. But after getting some perspective on my critical inner voices, I was ready to do something a lot more constructive.
>
> For the first time in my life, I felt like a strong and responsible adult taking charge of cleaning up the problems that needed to be resolved at work. My colleagues were impressed at how managerial and professional I was during this whole crisis. Once I took charge and became the leader of the clean-up effort, I realized there was no way I was going to be fired for what happened earlier. It was an honest mistake and it gave me a chance to show just how competent and devoted I really am.

If you are like Marjorie and you've grown up with highly critical parents or a bad case of perfectionism within yourself, now might be a crucial time to begin coming to terms with your Inner Critic. Only by taking control of these inner critical voices can you achieve your peak effectiveness at work.

As Marjorie described to me two months later when she came to her final therapy session:

I've spent my whole life worried that someone is going to expose me, find me out, or discover that I don't have what it takes. I've felt like that in my love relationships and I've felt it strongest at work.

But right now I feel a lot less anxious. I'm not second-guessing every move I make. By working on my internal critical voices, I've discovered that I don't have to keep living in fear all the time.

If someone at work is breathing down your neck and bombarding you with critical remarks, this is an excellent opportunity to do some internal work on how you respond to criticism and how you can manage your own Inner Critic. Don't let this opportunity slip by. Your emotional and physical health will be enhanced by whatever steps you take to come to terms with the critical voices you face at work.

8

Is Someone at Work Giving You the Cold Shoulder?

No one likes to be ignored. No one likes to be left out. Nor does it feel good to be treated like you don't exist.

Unfortunately, being left out or ignored is something we each have to deal with from time to time at work. Think about it for a moment. In the past few weeks or months, have you been frustrated because someone at work treated you in one of the following ways?

Getting left out of the loop. One of the games people play at work is the game of exclusion. Not inviting you to an important meeting. Not sending you a copy of an important memo. Not letting you know about an important situation. Keeping you in the dark about something that clearly affects your work and your well-being. Not including you in a social gathering where important conversations are happening.

Feeling an icy coldness from someone who used to be your warm ally or friend. Sometimes the most frustrating situation at work is when someone you once considered a supportive ally turns into a person who doesn't have the

161

time to be with you any longer or who has decided (for some office-politics reason) not to be close to you anymore. Even though you used to look forward to your work-related conversations with this individual, now something has changed. You are no longer friends or even allies. For some reason this person seems distant.

Having trouble getting a certain person to set aside time for you or your projects at work. It's hard to do your job well when someone whose input you clearly need will no longer make time to meet with you or refuses to treat your ideas and projects as a high priority.

It might be someone you work for who used to be easy to talk with and very accessible, but who now has become overworked or unavailable. This person always seems too busy now to pay attention to what you need from him or her.

Or it might be someone who's supposed to report to you but who now goes around you or ignores you on matters where you need full communication and cooperation. You feel like you're pulling teeth just to get this person to keep you informed on things you absolutely need to know about.

Or it might be someone who used to be a reliable customer, supplier, colleague, or coworker that you enjoyed working with and talking with. But now this person doesn't return your phone calls or memos. Or this person has changed somewhat and no longer supports the things you support. The two of you have grown distant and though you still run into one another in work settings, there's a lot of unresolved tension between you. The closeness is gone and a feeling of discomfort has replaced it.

"I Thought We Were Friends"

Trudi's story is a good example of what I mean by a Cold Shoulder.

An administrator for a large county agency, Trudi remembers three years ago when she needed to hire a public relations liaison and she called her old friend from college, whose name is Charlotte and who at that time was struggling to make ends meet as a free-lance publicist for nonprofit organizations.

As Trudi recalls, "I was so excited to be able to tell Charlotte about this job. Normally, our agency has to interview many candidates in a drawn-out process that can take months before they make a decision. But in this instance I knew Charlotte was right for the job. I introduced her to every important person at the agency and they liked her a lot. Because Charlotte was qualified for the position, and we really needed someone to start right away, my agency agreed with me that we should break precedent and hire her quickly without a long, wasteful search process."

For the first several months that they worked together, Trudi and Charlotte were not only friends outside of work but also allies in terms of office politics. According to Trudi, "There was this one administrator that I disliked tremendously and in the beginning Charlotte also found him obnoxious and unprofessional. We used to strategize together on how to deal with this guy. It was great having Charlotte as my friend and supporter whenever I was having difficulties with this other administrator."

But then something changed. Charlotte began to spend more time working on projects with the administrator who Trudi disliked so much. In addition, Charlotte began going skiing and playing golf with this administrator and several of his buddies. Trudi describes the change:

I could see where Charlotte would want to be nice to this guy. He did have a lot of clout at the agency and Charlotte's work in public relations necessitated that she get along with even the most obnoxious people. But it was more than that.

Charlotte and her new group of friends were very cliquish. You could sense at agency picnics and social events that they were the in group and that no one was welcome into their little social club. At one agency dinner I tried to sit next to Charlotte and I could see from the nervous look on her face that she wasn't completely comfortable having me there with her cliquish group of friends.

In addition to their distance on a social level, Trudi and Charlotte also had become adversaries in several important battles that had come up at their agency. Trudi explains:

Whenever there's a fight for control at the agency or a battle over who's going to get what share of the overall budget, Charlotte and I seem to be on different sides of the struggle. Charlotte and her cliquish friends always fight for whatever will preserve the status quo at the agency. Even if something's a mess, they don't want to fix it. On the other hand, I usually argue for the opposite side, hoping we can make some much-needed changes at the agency and improve things instead of sticking to the status quo.

At one recent meeting, Charlotte did something that really hurt me. There was a heated debate about the future direction of the agency. Charlotte happened to be facilitating that portion of the meeting and for a long time, she simply wouldn't call on me or even acknowledge that I was trying to get in on the conversation.

Then when I did get a chance to speak, Charlotte cut me off and turned the debate over to one of her cliquish friends who pulled a power play and got the top administrators to side with their point of view.

It wasn't just the frustration of getting ignored at that meeting. It was a much deeper hurt that Charlotte had treated me with so much coldness once again. I thought we were friends.

I realize, of course, that business is business. But Charlotte and I go way back. I still respect her intelligence and her creativity. I still look at her and it's hard not to think of her as a friend. I almost wanted to call her up on the phone and tell her how hurt I was after that meeting. But I didn't want to be that vulnerable with her. And besides, she and her group of friends all had victory smiles on their faces after that meeting. I can't let Charlotte find out how powerless I felt.

Why Is This Person Shunning You?

In previous chapters we were looking at difficult individuals who have a specific personality style that is unpleasant to work with—the Angry Screamer, the Saccharine Snake, the Space Case, or the Invalidator.

In this chapter we are dealing with something quite different. The person who is giving you the Cold Shoulder is not necessarily someone with an unpleasant or difficult personality. In fact, as Trudi found with her old friend Charlotte, you might still like or respect this person. If this individual weren't so busy or so caught up in office politics, it is likely you would still want to be this person's friend or ally.

With someone giving you the Cold Shoulder, the frustration is not because this individual is an obnoxious personality, but rather that your needs at work and this person's needs at work have begun to clash. Either because of a personal rivalry or some office politics, you are on different sides of the fence. The hurt is that you are being ignored and not taken seriously. If by some change of circumstance, you and this person were seeing eye to eye on something, there's a good chance you would be getting along fairly well.

But because of a specific clash between your needs and this person's needs, you are at odds with one another and you are being treated with coldness or disrespect. To better understand why you are being given the Cold Shoulder, consider the following three questions:

Question #1: What Changed?
If you want to discover the reasons why someone at work is ignoring you at crucial moments, you must find out what

specific thing changed the situation. Take a moment and recall:

- As you think back to your initial encounters with this person, do you remember when the two of you were getting along well?
- What changed?
- Did something change in the other person's workload or status at work that made him or her more anxious or rigid?
- Did something change in the other person's private life, personal health, or financial situation that made him or her more secretive or unapproachable?
- Was there an incident between you two that didn't get cleared up to the satisfaction of both of you?
- In what ways have your needs or styles of doing things begun to clash?

Question #2: Why Does the Other Person Feel the Need to Put Up a Wall or Keep You at a Distance?

The next step is to stop and consider why this person feels a need to give you (and possibly other people at work) the Cold Shoulder. By looking at the situation from his or her perspective, try to find out:

- Do you know what kind of person this individual was used to dealing with before you came on the scene?
- Were there clues early on that this individual was going to put up some barriers toward you or others?
- Is this individual in any way threatened by you or possibly is being rewarded at work for shutting you out of the loop?
- If you were in this person's shoes, would you have any reason to be keeping others out of your business?
- Do you know if you might possibly remind this individual of someone else—a parent, sibling, spouse, ex-spouse, boss, or ex-boss—who gave this individual a hard time?

Question #3: In What Way Did You Also Put Up a Wall and Feel the Need to Keep the Other Person at a Distance?

In most cases it is not just the other person who has changed. For a specific reason, you might also have put up some distance between the two of you.

Is there something about this person that irritates you or causes you to feel cold or distant? Does this person happen to remind you of someone else—a parent, sibling, spouse, ex-spouse, boss, or ex-boss—who gave you a hard time? Has something changed in your own work situation or in your private life that has made you a little more rigid or judgmental toward this other person? Is there something about the other person's style of doing things that you now find frustrating and as a result you have been feeling some tension between you?

To answer these questions, you probably will need to do more than just explore them on your own. There might be some information that can only be gained by talking with others.

For instance, to fully understand question #1 about what changed or question #2 about why the other person put up a wall, you probably need to speak to some of your coworkers or colleagues who have some additional insights about the situation. Possibly one of these coworkers or colleagues will know more about what changed for the other person or why he or she has put up some walls toward you.

This can be extremely useful if you have been taking something personally at work that doesn't need to be taken personally. For example, if you have been feeling slighted or rejected by someone and you do a little informal research with colleagues and coworkers, you might find you're not alone—other people at work also find this individual cold or distant.

Or you might be frustrated that a certain person at work doesn't return your phone calls or respond to your memos.

Your first reaction might be that this person doesn't like you or doesn't respect you. But if you do some informal research with colleagues and coworkers, you might discover that this individual has been out of town, has been ill recently, is getting transferred, is having a secretive affair, is getting divorced, or some other explanation that tells you, "Hey, stop taking all this so personally. The other person is putting up a wall for reasons that have nothing to do with you."

Trying to figure everything out on your own is a mistake, especially when the probability is high that the Cold Shoulder treatment you are receiving at work is similar or identical to the Cold Shoulder treatment that some of your colleagues or coworkers are receiving from this individual. The more you find out about the reasons behind the way you are being treated, the more clarity and self-respect you can gain for dealing with this frustrating situation.

Finding the Opportunity for a Heart-to-Heart Talk

You might also want to find a way to discuss with the actual person who has been giving you the Cold Shoulder exactly what has changed between the two of you. This is extremely important if you want to find a way to bridge the differences between you and become partners at work again.

You might feel reluctant at first to have a heart-to-heart talk with this other person. You might be harboring hurt feelings or resentments that are blocking you from finding out exactly why this person began to put up walls toward you. You might also have feelings of impatience or intolerance about this other person and you might be saying, "Why bother? Why bring this up with someone who's been ignoring me?"

This reluctance is quite common. For example, Trudi was extremely hesitant about having a heart-to-heart talk with her old friend Charlotte about their difficulties at work. As

Trudi explained to me, "It's much easier to put up my own wall toward Charlotte rather than try to find an opening in the wall she's put up toward me. What if I try to get closer to her again and she keeps pushing me away? That would be too frustrating."

So, like most of us who have been given the Cold Shoulder by someone at work, Trudi had made up her mind not to clear up her difficulties with Charlotte. Like most of us have done, Trudi resigned herself to seeing Charlotte almost daily at work but not speaking to her unless it was absolutely necessary.

Unfortunately, we each pay a high price for putting up walls at work. In Trudi's case, she discovered that becoming defensive and distant with Charlotte had the following drawbacks:

- They still needed to work together on several projects and the increased silence and distance between them were more uncomfortable than Trudi had anticipated.
- Trudi still respected and needed Charlotte's input and ideas on several important issues at work. By shutting Charlotte out of her life, Trudi no longer would benefit from Charlotte's creativity and professionalism.
- Trudi needed all the allies and support she could find to win some upcoming budget and priority fights at the agency. Even though Trudi was upset with Charlotte, she still needed Charlotte's support if it was possible to win Charlotte back as an ally on certain key issues.

For several weeks, Trudi and I discussed her mixed feelings about whether to have a heart-to-heart talk with Charlotte. On the one hand, Trudi wished the whole situation would disappear and that she never would have to talk with Charlotte again. On the other hand, Trudi knew that Charlotte was someone worth pursuing—if not as a close friend then at least as an important and influential colleague at work whose support could make or break some crucial projects.

Using her personal journal to write out her resentments and discuss them in her therapy sessions with me, Trudi took several weeks to work through her mixed feelings about Charlotte. Then she got up the courage and invited Charlotte to join her in what used to be an enjoyable activity—Sunday brunch at Trudi's favorite restaurant, followed by a long walk through one of the most beautiful parts of town. They had gone there together many times in the past, but the Sunday brunches stopped a few months earlier when their work relationship became strained.

As often happens when trying to set up a heart-to-heart talk with someone who's been giving you the Cold Shoulder, Trudi met some initial resistance from Charlotte. It took four phone calls and two cancelations before Trudi and Charlotte agreed on a date for having brunch together. As Trudi remembers:

> When Charlotte canceled for the second time, claiming she was too busy to take time off for a social engagement like brunch, I almost gave up on the whole thing. Why should I be civil to someone who is ignoring me like this? But we finally came up with a third date and time that Charlotte didn't cancel.
>
> At first I was tense and uncomfortable being alone with her in the restaurant. There was a part of me that wanted to say, ''Go to hell'' and storm out of there.
>
> I kept reminding myself that the reason I was there was to clear up some painful stuff with someone with whom I still have to work on a daily basis. So we started loosening up a bit and catching up on what's been going on in each of our lives since we last had the chance to be together.
>
> After a half hour of exchanging non-work–related stories, Charlotte began to feel like my old friend again. That's when I brought up our distance at work. I said, ''Charlotte, you and I have been on different sides of many issues at work. We disagree about certain people and certain political things at the office.

But I hope we can start over again and see if we can be allies with a lot less tension and a lot more of the old friendship. We don't need to agree on everything, but at least we can agree that we're two dynamite women who ought to support each other whenever possible.''

Trudi began to feel worried as soon as she had spoken these words. Would Charlotte push her away again or would there be some improvement in their work relationship? Trudi discovered,

To my surprise I saw a couple of tears in Charlotte's eyes and a look of concern on her face. She then admitted that she had missed my friendship as well.

Charlotte explained to me how hard it was for her to be acting businesslike and cold toward me during those months when we were clashing. She let me know that she'd gotten caught up in some of the unpleasant bullshit that goes with office politics at our agency. And she asked me if I would be willing to let her know in the future whenever I sensed we were drifting apart again.

Since that heart-to-heart talk, Trudi has found there are still some moments when Charlotte becomes a little bit distant and cold in work situations. There are also times when Charlotte gets caught up in some of the power games and cliquishness at the agency. But according to Trudi,

Even when Charlotte does something that irritates me, I know I can sit down with her and say, ''Hey jerkface, you're getting weird again. Can you pursue what you need to pursue without treating me like I'm your enemy? I'm not your enemy. I'm your friend, even when we disagree about things at work.''

Saying that to Charlotte usually starts a good conversation where she and I clear things up and strengthen our friendship. We still have our disagreements about certain people and issues at work, but now, even when we disagree, I still have the sense that Charlotte cares about me as a human being. That's the key.

A Time to Be Creative

There are some people who are a lot less easy to resolve things with than Charlotte was for Trudi. For example, you might be dealing with someone at work who gives you the Cold Shoulder and who would never be willing to join you for a Sunday brunch, a relaxing walk, or a heart-to-heart conversation.

You may need to take a different, more creative approach if you want to improve your work relationship with a highly inaccessible individual. Here are three possibilities that have proven successful for others in a similar situation.

Creative Possibility #1: Find a Conduit Person or a Mediator Who Has Clout to Urge This Individual to Stop Giving You the Cold Shoulder

Is there someone at work who would be willing to speak up to the person who's ignoring you and say, "Hey, let's not exclude (you)—. He or she ought to be consulted on this."

This conduit person can speak up on your behalf when you're not there to speak up for yourself. He or she can also find out for you why a certain individual is excluding you and what can be done to make sure the cold treatment doesn't continue.

In addition, the person at work who has a strong rapport with the individual who's been giving you the Cold Shoulder might also invite you to join them at an informal gathering where you will have a chance to clear things up. If you and the one giving you the Cold Shoulder have trouble communicating, this conduit person can serve as a mediator to help smooth out any miscommunications or other problems.

How to you find someone to play this role of the conduit or mediator? It's simple if you can identify someone at work who respects you and your work and who also has a strong relationship with the person who has been excluding you. You can ask for this person's help without being ashamed or apologetic. Simply say, "I need a favor. So and so is giving me the Cold Shoulder. You seem to be on good terms with both of us. Would you be willing to let me know whenever you see an opportunity for the three of us to get together and clean this up?"

I recently counseled a man named Barry who was being excluded from important meetings and crucial information by his supervisor, whose name is Warren. So Barry looked around his organization for someone who was respected and trusted by both Warren and himself. He identified a female colleague named Helena who was respected by Warren and who had worked closely with Barry on several successful projects. Barry decided to ask Helena for her support with Warren. During a meeting in Helena's office, Barry found a good moment and explained to Helena:

> I'm having a tough time working for Warren, mostly because he's extremely busy and he keeps leaving me out of important meetings and he doesn't keep me informed about details that I truly need for my work. So if you could help me, I'd appreciate you letting me know of any opportunities where I can be included in meetings or conversations that impact my work. And when I'm not included, if you could say something positive to Warren about my work or urge him to include me on important consultations, that would be great.

From asking Helena for her assistance, Barry discovered:

> There weren't any overnight changes. Warren still tended to make decisions on his own without consulting me and he usually didn't want anyone else from our department besides himself at certain meetings.

But then a few weeks after I asked Helena to be the conduit and speak up for me, something good happened. Helena and Warren were involved in some high-level meetings that lasted until almost 9 P.M. Warren was exhausted, and he complained to Helena that he'd been working too hard. Helena saw this as an opportunity to speak up on my behalf. She told Warren how much she liked my work and trusted my judgment on things. Then she asked Warren directly, "Why is it that you seem to exclude Barry from important meetings?"

Warren was surprised to have someone like Helena touting the work of one of his employees. At first he didn't say much, commenting only, "I figure Barry has enough to do without being required to attend these awful meetings." But when the next planning meeting was announced, Warren came into my office and told me he wanted to make sure I was involved in more of these sessions.

Without much trouble, Helena had gotten the job done. She'd put the idea in Warren's head to start including me more. Over the next few months, there were still times when Warren was too busy or too secretive to keep me informed on certain things. But overall, he's improved a great deal. I get invited to meetings far more often than previously and I'm consulted much more now than I was before Helena acted on my behalf.

Can you identify someone where you work who would be willing to be your conduit or mediator, to speak up on your behalf to the person who's been giving you the Cold Shoulder?

If you can't come up with someone immediately, then you might need to look for someone from personnel, human resources, or employee relations to speak up on your behalf. No one has the right to keep excluding you or ignoring you on matters that impact your effectiveness at work. Make sure you find someone who can put the idea of including you more often into the mind of the person who has been giving you the Cold Shoulder.

Creative Possibility #2: Find a Moment When This Person Really Needs Your Input or Your Information, and Then Make Sure You Get an Agreement That in the Future You Will be Included More Often

Timing is important. If you sit down and talk with someone who has been giving you the Cold Shoulder, you might find two different reactions based on the timing of your conversation. If this happens to be a moment when this individual really needs your input or your information, then you have some clout to ask him or her for more inclusion in the future. If this happens to be a moment when this individual doesn't really need your input or your information, then you may be at risk for more rejection if you insist on more inclusion at that moment.

Fortunately, you get to control when you pick your moment to assert yourself with someone who has been giving you the Cold Shoulder. Be sure to look for a moment when this individual truly needs you and your ideas or suggestions. Knowing that this is your best chance to be taken seriously by this individual, seize the opportunity and be professional in the way you present your information.

Most importantly, take a brief pause before or after giving this person the information he or she needs. Stop and look the person directly in the eye as you say, ''I've noticed lately that it's hard to find time for the two of us to consult with one another on things like this that impact our work. We need to set up a definite time to make sure we don't keep missing out on what we could be offering each other.''

Notice that these words do not accuse and are less of a criticism than they are an invitation for the two of you to improve things at work. There is no point in criticizing or attacking someone who's been giving you the Cold Shoulder; that would probably make the other person even more distant and inaccessible. On the other hand, if you seize the correct moment and you make sure to sound professional and valuable, you stand a much better chance of getting this person to take you seriously.

For example, Carey is the manager of a department that needs to consult with many other departments at his company. But quite often Carey finds he can't get certain department heads to schedule time to meet with him. With one particular department head, whose name is Brenda, there have been repeated cancelations of appointments. Even though Carey's work is sometimes essential to Brenda's department, Brenda keeps canceling meetings with Carey and saying, "I'm just too busy to meet with you now. This will have to wait until things calm down."

According to Carey, "When she says I'll have to wait until things calm down, I realize that's the same as never. Brenda hasn't been willing to sit down and meet with me or anyone in my department for far too long."

For the next few days, Carey waited patiently until the right moment to try creative possibility #2. Then the opportunity arrived. Someone in Carey's department had prepared an extremely important research study that had significant repercussions for Brenda and her department. Carey knew this was the moment to take a chance and attempt to bring up the fact that Brenda had been giving his department the Cold Shoulder for much too long a time.

Carey sent Brenda a confidential memo that said,

Very important research findings could impact your department. Want to discuss strategies with you. Call when you're ready to set up a sixty-minute meeting to discuss this and some other important issues.

Carey describes what happened next.

As I should have known, Brenda didn't take the bait. Yes, this was a crucial research study, but no, she wasn't going to schedule sixty of her precious minutes to meet with me. She called and left a message, saying, "Too busy to meet. Just send me the research."

Carey knew, however, that this was his best chance to force a meeting with Brenda and bring up several unaddressed issues that she had been putting off for months. So he called her back and said, "We need to talk before I let anyone else see the research study. How about today before lunch?"

By the time Brenda returned his phone call, it was almost noon. She told Carey, "I can see you for ten minutes in my office."

Carey was almost tempted to settle for only ten minutes of her time, but then he stopped himself and said, "No, this will take at least a half hour. I'll order lunch. Do you want Italian or Thai?"

Brenda still wouldn't budge. She replied, "No, I've got some work I have to catch up on during lunch. All I can give you is ten minutes and that's a stretch right now."

Carey didn't back down. He commented, "Brenda, this is something important, and I think you're going to want to hear me explain the ramifications and some of the alternatives that could make it a win for you and your department."

Brenda thought for a moment and then said, "Oh what the hell. I'll order Chinese food and you bring the report."

During their working lunch, Carey and Brenda not only had an excellent conversation spelling out the issues raised by the current research study, but they also cleared up several other pieces of business that had been pushed aside in the past few months.

Carey recalls the lunch meeting:

It was a breakthrough. First, because Brenda got to see that I'm not trying to waste her time. There are important things that I need to discuss about her department and she could see that I'm not some jerk who schedules meetings for no good reason.

Second, I got to see how she works and why she tends to be as unapproachable as she is. I realized for the first time that she's not giving me the Cold Shoulder to be mean or difficult. She truly has a huge overload of work and responsibilities. I've got to admire the fact that she refuses to let anyone waste her time with nonessential meetings or chitchat.

As we ate some excellent Chinese food that she'd ordered, I could tell that she was definitely impressed with how I'd analyzed this research and its implications for her department. So right at the moment when I could see she knew I wasn't there to waste her time, I told her that in the future I'd make sure not to bother her on any nonessential issues. But that if I did call her and say I needed thirty or sixty minutes of her time, that meant it was important and she ought to find a way to schedule some time.

By the end of our lunch, I had the feeling that we understood each other a lot better. I know not to bother her with anything trivial and she knows that I'm professional and serious. So when I need to discuss something with her, she's open to hearing what I have to say.

Creative Possibility #3: Use This Incident with Someone Giving You the Cold Shoulder as an Opportunity to Resolve Your Own Issues About Being Snubbed or Neglected by Someone You've Counted On

Most human beings grow up with some painful experiences regarding the issue of being left out, ignored, or rejected. For some people, the painful experience was that one or both of their parents were emotionally unavailable at crucial times. For others, the painful moments happened when someone they loved or were attracted to romantically suddenly became cold or distant or rejecting. Still others have had painful experiences of being left out of social cliques in junior high or high school, or of being excluded from important groups in college or in their careers.

Whatever the source of the painful memories, these hurts are easily retriggered when someone at work is giving you the Cold Shoulder. Even if you think that the painful incidents are long forgotten in the past, all it takes is a frustrating situation with someone at work ignoring you or excluding you and these emotions from long ago can flare up inside you.

How do you handle these painful reminders of times in your past when you were rejected or excluded? How do you make sure that you don't act inappropriately at work because someone in the present is doing something that retriggers old hurts from the past?

There are some clues you can watch for that might tell you that the person giving you the Cold Shoulder at work has retriggered old hurts from the past. For instance, ask yourself:

- Do you sometimes feel preoccupied with thoughts about the person who has been giving you the Cold Shoulder?
- Do you ever lie awake at night planning your next move to get this person to take you seriously?
- Whenever you see this individual working with or talking with someone else, do you notice yourself resenting it?
- Do you feel as though this person has singled you out and is ignoring you more than he or she ignores anyone else?
- Do you get unusually anxious or tongue-tied around this person who has been ignoring you?
- Do you find yourself having conversations in your mind with this person, hoping to convince him or her that you are worthy or valuable and deserve better treatment?
- Are you sometimes so frustrated by the Cold Shoulder treatment that you actually avoid dealing with this individual, even at times when he or she is available?

• Do you feel that you are putting up your guard to protect yourself from this person's rejection, even when this person is interested in working with you or talking with you?

If two or more of the above questions ring true for you, there's a good chance that the current situation with someone giving you the Cold Shoulder at work has restimulated some old hurts from your past. Now might be a good time to talk with a close friend or a therapist, or to write in your private journal and sort out these complex feelings. You can begin to work through the emotional issues by answering these questions:

• When in the past have you experienced the same kind of exclusion or inaccessibility that you now experience with this individual at work?
• In the past, what did you try to do to protect yourself against similar incidents? Did you withdraw and become secretive, did you run away, or did you smile as though this person's rejecting you wasn't affecting you?
• What have you done in the past at work when someone gave you the Cold Shoulder or excluded you from something important?
• Have you ever been able to get someone who was excluding you at work to start taking you seriously? What have you tried that was effective or ineffective?

By working on these questions with a good friend, a therapist, or in your private journal, you are essentially taking a crucial step forward in your life. Instead of continuing to feel victimized and powerless when someone is ignoring you or excluding you, you will begin to sort out what your constructive options are for dealing with situations like these. Even if you were truly powerless to improve the way you were treated by someone long ago who ignored you or rejected you, now there might be a far greater chance of dealing more effectively with the situation. But first you need to work through your unresolved emotions about being given the Cold Shoulder in general.

Meredith's case is a good illustration of what I mean by using the incident of someone giving you the Cold Shoulder as an opportunity for resolving your own issues about being snubbed or neglected by someone you've counted on.

Since Meredith works as a free-lance artists' representative, she has to meet new people constantly in order to sell the artwork of her clients. As a result, she often must deal with situations where she gets rejected, ignored, or is given the Cold Shoulder. Yet, because of Meredith's childhood experiences, getting ignored or excluded has always been an extremely painful issue for her.

At a recent art opening, Meredith was introduced to the art buyer for a major real estate developer. At first Meredith thought this buyer, whose name is Sylvianne, was going to be an outstanding contact for her clients. But after a few weeks of doing business together, Meredith found that Sylvianne suddenly became cold and unavailable. When Meredith would leave messages, Sylvianne didn't return the calls. When Meredith got Sylvianne on the phone, the buyer seemed impatient and always too busy to talk.

After Meredith attended one of my weekend workshops on winning at office politics, she told me privately,

> For some reason, I can't seem to just accept the fact that Sylvianne is giving me the Cold Shoulder and that it's normal for that to happen in business. I've been able to rationalize lots of rejections in the past, but this one has begun to preoccupy me. I'm mulling it over in my mind for far too long each day. I'm having conversations in my head where I try to convince Sylvianne that she ought to be taking me and my artists more seriously. I'm feeling victimized whenever she's too busy to talk to me. It's not a pleasant way to live.

In addition to feeling somewhat preoccupied by the Cold Shoulder treatment from Sylvianne, Meredith also described to me how anxious and tongue-tied she had become whenever she called Sylvianne on the phone or ran into her at a gallery event.

Meredith admitted,

Even though I have some artists who are perfect for Sylvianne's projects, I get so bottled up with anxiety when I'm about to pitch Sylvianne with any of these clients of mine. I'm not usually like this and it's frustrating that someone who is being cold and distant toward me can make me feel so powerless and insecure.

Over the next several weeks, Meredith and I began to explore what in her past experiences might be causing her preoccupation and her anxiousness toward Sylvianne. As often happens when someone giving you the Cold Shoulder causes a painful aftereffect that you can't dismiss easily, Meredith had several incidents in her past that had been retriggered by Sylvianne's coldness toward her.

First, Meredith, like many seemingly well-adjusted adults, had tried to ignore the fact that as a child she often felt insecure or left out in social situations. An only child raised by two highly educated parents, Meredith recalls growing up in a family where, "My parents could go on and on talking to each other and completely leave me out. Or if I did get a word in, it usually sounded less intelligent or less interesting than what they were talking about."

As a teenager in junior high school, Meredith had become even more sensitive to being an outsider or being ignored when in eighth grade her family moved to a different neighborhood and Meredith had to try to break into the already-established cliques at her school. Meredith remembers feeling, "No matter what I did, they always treated me like an unwelcome outsider."

That feeling of being ignored or left out also repeated

itself in one of Meredith's first jobs after college. She explains, "I was hired to be part of a sales organization that prided itself not on how well you treated your customers but on how aggressively you met your monthly quotas. When I would attend sales meetings or company retreats, I was so isolated from all the other sales reps. It was as though I was the only humanistic fool in a sea of ruthless sharks. After two years at that company, I felt absolutely insecure about whether my warm, personal style in business was going to be an asset or a terrible liability."

During our therapy sessions, Meredith gradually came to terms with the fact that she had been struggling for most of her life with deep feelings of not being included and not being taken seriously. With so much exclusion in her background is it any wonder that the Cold Shoulder treatment from someone like Sylvianne would make her feel insecure and tongue-tied?

In addition, Meredith discovered during one of our sessions that Sylvianne was a lot like Meredith's mother, especially in the way Sylvianne seemed so interested one moment in what Meredith was saying and then suddenly seemed completely inaccessible in the next moment.

Over the next several weeks, Meredith practiced staying calm when she called or visited Sylvianne by reassuring herself each time and saying, "This woman is not my mother. Nor is she trying to ignore me or hurt me. She's simply a customer of mine who has an odd way of keeping her distance."

As a result of her therapy sessions and her ability to say comforting things like that to herself when she was about to pitch Sylvianne for one of her artist clients, Meredith soon regained her ability to feel strong and professional when dealing with Sylvianne. Within a relatively short time, she was no longer tongue-tied or overly anxious when selling to Sylvianne.

In addition, something interesting happened for Meredith that often happens when someone resolves their hurts from the past in order to be more effective with someone giving them the Cold Shoulder in the present. Because of Meredith's willingness to do inner work on her past experiences with feeling ignored or rejected, she began appearing far more relaxed and comfortable in each conversation with Sylvianne. Gradually, Sylvianne noticed the change in Meredith. Instead of seeming to be a nervous and insecure sales representative, Meredith began to seem more like an intelligent ally, a welcome friend, and someone to whom Sylvianne could confide.

Over a period of months, Meredith and Sylvianne began to see each other occasionally at social events and would let one another know about upcoming art events. What had begun as an intimidating and anxiety-ridden work relationship had progressed into a personal friendship and an outstanding source of business for Meredith's artist clients. Whenever Sylvianne needed artwork for a new or remodeled real estate project, she relied first and foremost on Meredith's artists.

While not every situation in which someone is giving you the Cold Shoulder turns into a friendship like the one developed between Meredith and Sylvianne, in most cases you can still expect a great deal of improvement from doing the inner work described above. Not only will you feel less anxious and tongue-tied around the other person, but your sense of professionalism and self-worth will also be enhanced. Instead of being intimidated by someone you work with on a regular basis, you will feel a lot more adult and competent even if this person continues to treat you with some degree of coldness and inaccessibility.

9

How to Deal with a Testosteroni

In the comedy film *Frankie and Johnny,* a waitress named Frankie (played by Michelle Pfeiffer) is asked by another waitress to help her handle a male customer who thinks he has the right to grab the behind of any woman who serves him food.

Quickly, Michelle Pfeiffer's character tells the other waitress, "You pour. I'll bump."

Pretending a collision, they drench ice water on the man's crotch.

If dealing with a Testosteroni at work were always as simple as that, you wouldn't need to read the following pages. Unfortunately, it's not simple. How to respond to certain men at work who are run by their hormones is something about which we all need to learn a lot more.

A Brief History of a Very Complicated Issue

A few decades ago, sexual harassment and gender discrimination were overt and there was almost nothing you could do about it. A boss could say to an employee, "Go to bed with me or else you're fired." A colleague could comment on your private parts or call you honey or doll in a demeaning way and there was nothing you could do except smile or quit.

If a promotion was kept from you because of your gender, your only recourse was to put up with the unfairness or else resign. If you faced a hostile situation day after day at work in which someone treated you badly because of their patronizing attitude toward women, all you could do was tolerate it or leave.

In certain aspects, some progress has been made in the past twenty years. There are now laws, procedures, agencies, and successful strategies that never existed before to protect you against being mistreated by someone whose hormones are on overdrive. There are thousands of people who have filed and won sexual harassment and discrimination claims. There are dozens of organizations that actively watch for workplace discrimination, as well as giving support and advice to people who are mistreated because of their gender.

What Hasn't Gotten Better

In certain other respects, the situation has not improved nearly enough. Even though sexual harassment and gender bias in the 1990s are less socially permissible than they were a few decades ago, these forms of mistreatment still remain widespread.

A sexually hormonal boss in the "politically correct" 1990s usually won't come right out and say, "Go to bed with me or else you're fired." These days, an aroused boss is more likely to say, "I'm your mentor, I'm your friend, I care about your professional growth here, and I'm the one person you can trust (so go to bed with me)."

In this era of lawsuits and social awareness, a discriminatory boss won't come right out and say, "We didn't promote you to that spot because you're a woman and we get nervous about having too many women in powerful positions.''

Instead, a company will hire expensive lawyers and public relations experts to help them defend in a lengthy trial why they are underpaying their most qualified female employees or failing to promote them above a certain level.

But even the U.S. Labor Department now admits there is a glass ceiling in corporate America, in which women can look up and see the top corporate jobs but they are blocked in most cases from getting there. In 1991 the Labor Department released an extensive study of just how difficult it is for qualified women to break through the glass ceiling that still exists at the vast majority of U.S. corporations.

An Issue Whose Time Has Come

Most women today don't need experts and studies to tell them there is still a lot of harassment and discrimination in the workplace. You can feel it in your gut when you are being treated in a condescending way. You can tell if a man (or a woman for that matter) is acting strangely toward you because he or she isn't comfortable working with an assertive woman. You can sense it intuitively if you are involved in a business interaction with a man who looks at each woman as nothing more than a potential conquest. You can hear it in the hostile jokes, remarks, and stories that are told constantly in work environments, even in the ''enlightened'' 1990s.

I call this chapter ''How to Deal with a Testosteroni'' not because I am anti-male (I happen to be male). Nor do I assume that there are no instances in which sexual harassment and job discrimination take place against men. There are situations in which men get mistreated at work based on their gender and this chapter can be helpful to any males who suffer from those injustices.

But most of the time in our society the problem is how

certain men—because of their hormones, their upbringing, or the society we live in—treat the women with whom they work.

In my definition, a Testosteroni is someone who doesn't know when to stop pushing. If he's attracted to you and you say no, he doesn't want to believe that you truly mean no. A Testosteroni seems to enjoy the fact that when a woman at work is confronted by sexual requests or sexist remarks, she is being placed in an unfairly vulnerable position. A Testosteroni can also be someone who simply doesn't want to treat a female colleague with respect or equality. No matter how smart or qualified a woman at work might be, a Testosteroni still views her either as a threat or as someone who is there to service his needs and his fantasies.

Sexual discrimination and harassment in the workplace is an issue whose time has come. Not only does a Testosteroni make life miserable for the women he mistreats, but his hormonal urges also have some hidden costs for the companies involved. According to a 1988 survey of Fortune 500 companies, ignoring the issue of sexual harassment and discrimination costs a typical Fortune 500 company as much as $6.7 million a year in absenteeism, turnover, and lost productivity. That's a lot of wasted money and talent because some horny fellows can't keep their urges under control.

What Exactly Is Against the Law?

Let's say a man you work for tells you he wants to see you socially and he admits he fantasizes about you sometimes. What if you tell him you're not interested in going out with him and then he keeps asking you for a date or he starts treating you coldly at business meetings?

Part of the problem in dealing with a Testosteroni is that you might not be sure how to assess the seriousness of what this person is doing. Should his sexual interest be taken as a compliment? Should it be seen as a danger sign that you are no longer being treated as a secure employee but rather as a would-be girlfriend whose career might be in jeopardy if the relationship goes sour?

How will you be sure if saying no to this man is not going to affect your future raises, promotions, or professional treatment? Has your working environment or your ability to do your job been compromised by this man's sexual pursuit of you?

How do you respond to his come-on without appearing to be harsh or cruel? What if saying no doesn't get the message across to him? What if you need this guy for a reference later?

In order to respond to a Testosteroni, you first must be sure in your own mind that what he is doing is inappropriate. Based on my interviews with employment law specialists and human resources experts, I have found that there are several clues you can look for that indicate a male colleague has crossed the line and gone past the respectful compliment zone to the danger zone of sexual harassment or discrimination. See if any of the following are taking place where you work and are putting you in an uncomfortable dilemma.

Unwelcome advances and requests for sexual favors. There are two types of advances that cross the line. First, if you are told or if it is implied that sexual compliance is expected of you as part of your employment, that is blatant harassment.

In addition, there is a second type of harassment, of which many people are unaware, that also crosses the line. If someone's sexual remarks or advances create an intimidating, hostile, or offensive working environment in which a "reasonable woman" feels mistreated or that her work situation has been comprised, then this, too, can be legally pursued as unwelcome sexual harassment.

You should be aware that in recent years the courts have decided that the point of view of a "reasonable woman" is what counts in sexual harassment cases. Whereas a man might view some sexual remark as innocent fun, if a woman finds it creates a hostile environment, then the woman's point of view is crucial. Note that this "reasonable woman" criterion, proposed by the Ninth Circuit Court of Appeals in the 1991 case of *Ellison* v. *Brady*, is still being debated by judges and legal scholars. Always consult an attorney before taking any formal action in a sexual harassment case.

In addition to sexual advances, there are many other clues that sexual harassment or discrimination have crossed the line. They include:

Actual or threatened retaliation against a person who complains or intends to complain of sexual harassment or discrimination. Whereas twenty years ago a company could intimidate someone into keeping quiet, now a company might be liable if they say or do things that threaten the job security or the personal well-being of someone who is speaking up against harassment or discrimination.

Hiring or promotion practices that set up unfair obstacles against women. If you can prove that you are qualified and yet you are being excluded from a good job primarily because you are a woman, there are now many legal precedents to support you in taking action against your employer.

Pay scales that subtly discriminate against jobs that are traditionally done by women. Even though it may be harder to prove, some women have successfully shown that by paying certain male-dominated positions a higher salary for comparable work than certain female-dominated positions, an environment of discrimination and unfairness has been practiced. Every time a company is forced to pay men and women comparable wages for comparable jobs, this disparity between what women and men earn for similar work is decreased.

Visual displays that create a hostile working environment. A 1991 decision in the Middle District of Florida

(*Robinson* v. *Jacksonville Shipyards*) found that a female shipyard welder was justified in claiming sexual harassment because she had to work in an environment where there were prominently displayed calendar pictures of women in various stages of undress as well as some demeaning remarks by male employees and supervisors. The court ruled that this working environment was hostile and intimidating because it created an atmosphere of sexual stereotyping (women as sexual toys) that made it unfairly difficult for women employees there to be treated fairly and could also lead to a biased job performance evaluation of women who complain about the atmosphere or who act inconsistently with the stereotype.

Verbal comments or nonverbal gestures that are inappropriate in a professional working relationship. If someone repeatedly comments on your body parts, grabs you, or looks you up and down in a way that makes you uncomfortable, those actions could be creating a hostile work environment. Or if someone compliments you in an inappropriate way such as, ''I wish my wife were as pretty as you,'' or ''I wonder what you're like in bed,'' it might undermine a professional working relationship. Or if someone refers to you as honey, sweetheart, or babe, even though you've made it clear that you don't appreciate those belittling terms, then you might be justified in saying that this person is not respecting you as an adult professional colleague.

The intent of these rules on sexual harassment and discrimination is not to punish what a man thinks in his own private fantasies, but rather to make sure his private sexual thoughts and stereotypes are kept out of the workplace so they don't interfere with a female colleague who is trying to do her job.

What to Do in Response

Even if your first reaction is to keep your mouth shut and pretend nothing happened, there are several important actions you need to take in order to protect yourself against harassment or discrimination by a powerful Testosteroni.

Get support from a colleague. Make sure you tell someone what this person did that was uncomfortable or confusing to you. You need to have someone who is on your side. You deserve to have someone who knows what happened and who takes it seriously. You might at some point need this person to testify on your behalf. You also deserve to have someone who supports you emotionally and knows you don't deserve to have your job security threatened by someone's inappropriate behavior.

Document exactly what happened. Keep a written record of each incident, times, dates, locations, what happened, and who said what. Also make note of any witnesses who saw or heard what happened or any nearby people who might have seen you or the other person walking away from the incident. Make sure you document anything you might have said or done to let the Testosteroni know that you aren't comfortable with his desires or actions.

If possible, tell a supervisor or an employee relations manager as soon as you can unless, of course, this is the person mistreating you, in which case you need to find someone else you can ask for help. Find out if your company has a specific policy against sexual harassment or discrimination, and what procedures must be followed. Find out if there are other complaints against this individual. Find out what your company will or won't do. Find out what is the deadline or statute of limitations for filing a formal complaint. Make written notes of each of these conversations with company personnel.

Most importantly, let the Testosteroni know that your answer is no and that you take your job seriously. If you feel clear enough to tell this person immediately that you are not comfortable with his sexual remarks or discriminatory behavior, be sure to do so and then document in writing exactly what you said and what the person responded.

If you don't feel comfortable saying it in person, then write a letter to this individual. Detail exactly what specific behavior you want stopped and what actions you will take if the behavior continues. Make sure to date and sign this letter and keep a copy of it for yourself. You can also bring a witness along with you when you give a copy to the Testosteroni.

In some situations, you might feel that your job or your personal safety are threatened by having to confront this individual. In that case, make sure you get the support of someone at work who understands what you are going through. You do not have to do this all by yourself. Your friends will want to help you. The human resources department has an implied duty to make sure your rights are protected. In fact, anyone at your company who understands the seriousness of sexual harassment and discrimination will also appreciate that you need a lot of support at this time.

If you don't have this kind of professional support at work or if the person mistreating you won't stop the behavior despite your making it clear that you want it stopped, then you can also file a complaint with the State Department of Fair Employment or with the Federal Equal Employment Opportunity Commission. This will lead to an investigation of your claim. If the agency finds that your claim is justified, they will begin formal hearings on your behalf. If you find that these governmental agencies are taking too long or are not responding to your situation, you can consult an attorney and file a lawsuit as well. In most cases, these agency claims and lawsuits are settled out of court. However, you should always be prepared for a lengthy process and you should document as much evidence as possible along the way to support your side of the dispute.

Why Most Testosteronis Are Never Confronted

Even though our legal system clearly states that sexual harassment and discrimination are not permissible in the workplace, most women and men are reluctant to report it. Just as an intelligent and legally knowledgeable woman like Anita Hill kept her problems with Clarence Thomas silent for almost ten years, so do most victims of harassment and discrimination suffer silently without taking action.

Why is this so? Why is it far more likely that a person would rather put up with stomach problems, tension headaches, or other stress-related symptoms than to speak up against an employer or colleague who is disrupting her work life with his inappropriate behaviors? Why do women who have a tremendous amount of self-confidence and courage still feel unable to go public about discrimination or sexual abusiveness in the workplace? Even today, when the subject has been discussed on every talk show from Oprah to Phil to Geraldo to Sally, why is it still so hush-hush?

Clearly there is a lot of emotional turmoil involved in a sexual harassment or discrimination case that must be understood in order to find out why most Testosteronis are never confronted. Certainly there is an explanation why millions of women claim in scientific surveys that they have been harassed at work, yet only a small percentage of that number have reported these incidents to personnel departments or to state or federal authorities.

From my experience over the past several years counseling people in sexual harassment and discrimination cases, I have found that there are three psychological reasons why most people keep silent, thus enabling the Testosteroni to get away with his inappropriate behavior. Only by understanding these powerful psychological forces can you make a healthy decision as to how you will respond to your own difficult situation at work:

Psychological Factor #1: Are You Blaming Yourself for Someone Else's Inappropriateness?

Have you ever felt guilty for something that wasn't your fault? I have found that in seven out of ten sexual harassment incidents the woman being harassed says to herself at some point, "I must have done something wrong to be treated like this."

She starts wondering, "What did I do to provoke this guy? Was it something I said? Was it something about the way I was dressed? Should I stop wearing perfume? Should I stop being so friendly to people I work with?"

Even if the woman has been acting in a strictly professional fashion and hasn't done anything that should have sparked the persistent harassment she has been receiving, she still is likely to feel worried and uncertain about whether she is somehow to blame.

I recently counseled a woman named Margo who was having problems at work with a boss who kept assuring her that he was her mentor and her friend; at the same time he kept trying to start an affair with her even though he is married.

Margo felt burdened and confused by his constant sexual remarks to her. Should she keep silent and hope he stops? Should she quit her job to get away from his persistent efforts to lure her? Should she speak up against her powerful boss?

One of Margo's issues in therapy was that she, like many people, tended to feel guilty and blame herself for things that were not her fault. If a close friend didn't call Margo for a few weeks, Margo's first reaction was to worry and ask herself, "I wonder if I said something that upset my friend."

Or if Margo had a business appointment and the other person failed to show up, Margo's first thought would often be, "I must have gotten the time wrong. I probably made a mistake."

In both of these situations, Margo was not at fault. Yet her strong sense of responsibility had made her worry that she had been the cause of her friend not calling or that somehow Margo had been at fault for the business associate not showing up for their meeting.

So when Margo's boss kept making sexual advances at her, Margo's tendency to feel responsible and guilty had her wondering, "Am I at fault for his sexual interest in me? Am I somehow teasing this guy or giving out a sexual vibe? Should I stop wearing fashionable clothing or the perfume my sister bought me for my birthday?"

Like many caring and considerate human beings, Margo found it easier to blame herself and feel guilty than to speak up against her boss's sexual advances. As she told me during one of her counseling sessions:

> I feel trapped by my boss coming on to me time after time. On the one hand, I wish he'd stop so I can go back to doing my job again without having to worry about his making these demands on me. On the other hand, I notice that there are lots of good looking women in the office and he doesn't seem to be hitting on them. So maybe there's something about the way I'm being too friendly or too caring that's giving him the wrong message.

Does this sound like you or anyone you know? Have you noticed that you've begun to question your appearance, your friendliness, or your own sexuality as a result of someone making sexual remarks or advances toward you at work? Are you worrying about whether you might somehow be encouraging the aggressive come-ons from a certain individual? Are you finding it difficult to focus on your job because there is so much unspoken tension between you and this person at work?

I have found in most sexual harassment cases, the woman being harassed is not doing anything inappropriate. Even though it is common to feel guilty or to wonder if somehow you are encouraging the Testosteroni who can't seem to take no for an answer, there are some crucial facts you need to consider.

There is no crime in looking good, dressing well, wearing perfume, or being friendly at your job. Just as men have the right to look their best and be friendly to anyone at work who is an important business contact, so do women have the right to look their best and be friendly at work to any business contact without being accused of being flirtatious or a tease.

If a woman is friendly or caring to a male colleague or boss at work, it is usually not an invitation for sexual come-ons or accusatory remarks. If a man isn't mature enough to realize that an attractive woman at work is there to make a living and not to fulfill his sexual fantasies, then this man has a problem that could be interfering with the productivity and job performance of the women with whom he works.

If a man misinterprets a woman's aliveness or friendliness and he sees it as a sexual invitation when in fact it's not, then he needs to be professional enough to realize that one "no" should be sufficient to tell him to stop his sexual advances.

In Margo's case, it took a while for her to stop blaming herself and start realizing that her boss was the person who was being highly unprofessional. Margo was not being sexually provocative to her boss, even though she needed to be friendly and caring in order to do her job. Nor was she being sexually enticing when she dressed well or wore expensive perfume to the office. She had the right to look good and feel good without blaming herself for the fact that her boss was unable to control his sexual wishes when working in close proximity to someone as competent and alive as Margo.

When Margo's boss continued to press her for sex and he refused to let her do her job without this harassment, Margo had to make a decision. Could she speak up against her boss and insist that he stop this illegal and unprofessional conduct? She now knew that his sexual come-ons were not because of any inappropriate actions on her part. She no longer blamed herself. But she still felt anxious about forcing him to stop. This brings us to the second difficulty faced by most women in dealing with a Testosteroni.

Psychological Factor #2: Is There a Substantial Power Imbalance Between You and the Person Mistreating You?

In most sexual harassment and discrimination cases, the reason why people keep silent is not because they don't feel angry or upset with the mistreatment. It's because they feel a huge power imbalance—they tend to feel powerless compared to the person who's using sexuality or gender in an intimidating way.

It's easier to imagine speaking up against a peer or subordinate who mistreats you at work than it is to imagine speaking up against a boss or very important customer or colleague. To illustrate this issue of power imbalances and how it silences people, here is an exercise developed by psychologist Michele Paludi of New York's Hunter College to help men and women understand the dynamics of sexual harassment in the workplace. I have revised this exercise and used it successfully in workshops I have given on this topic. See what your reactions are.

- Imagine that you are highly allergic to smoke and you enter an elevator at work where someone is smoking. How would you deal with this situation?

    In most cases, people say they would speak up. Some would keep silent and others would try to get out of the elevator as soon as possible without making a scene. But the majority feel pretty sure they would say something if they were trapped in a confining elevator with a smoker and they were allergic to smoke.

- Now imagine that the person smoking in the elevator is the most powerful person where you work, or the most important customer or colleague you know. Imagine that it's your boss or some other powerful individual who has the clout to fire you or hurt you economically. How would you deal with this situation? Would you speak up, would you wait for a chance to escape, or would you just keep silent?

  In most cases, even the people who say they would speak up in general now find they are much less likely to speak up when the exercise deals with someone powerful or important who could affect your finances or your future.

If you take into account this natural tendency to keep silent when there is a huge power imbalance between you and the person mistreating you, then you can understand why Anita Hill and most others have been reluctant to speak up for many years about harassment and gender discrimination. But at the same time, there are things you can do to reduce the power imbalance and make it possible for your side of the dispute to be just as important and well-supported as the other person's.

In Margo's case, once she stopped blaming herself and realized that her boss was the one who was acting in an inappropriate and illegal fashion, the challenge became how to speak up without jeopardizing her job security or her career. How could she speak up to someone who had the power to fire her or make her life miserable? How would she take steps to counteract the power imbalance between herself and the person mistreating her?

For Margo to get her boss to stop his persistent harassment, I advised her to take the following action steps:

1. She spoke with an attorney to find out exactly what her options were if she decided to file a formal complaint.
2. Margo invited several of her closest friends from work out to lunch where she asked for their emotional support on this issue. She also asked her friends to keep her situation a secret until she gave them further notice.
3. Margo pulled together all the documentation and written evidence she had been compiling for several weeks about her boss's sexual pressuring of her.
4. She arranged for a meeting with her company's director of human resources to discuss what the company policy was for dealing with sexual harassment claims. At that meeting, the human resources director could see how extensive Margo's documentation was. It was clear Margo could pursue and possibly win a sexual harassment claim if her situation wasn't resolved successfully in-house by the human resources department.
5. Margo and the director of human resources met with Margo's boss and informed him that his harassment had to stop immediately and that any continued harassment or retaliation by him would have serious consequences.

You will notice in Margo's case that the imbalance of power was significantly reduced once she had gotten her attorney, her friends, her documentation, and her director of human resources all on her side. In some cases, that resolves the problem. The Testosteroni backs off. It's not pleasant to have to keep working in close proximity to someone you've confronted, but in Margo's case, she strongly desired to keep her job and not be transferred to a less familiar department. Nor did she feel it was necessary to have her boss transferred. As she told the human resources director at the time,

All I care about is that the sexual remarks have got to stop. I can work with my boss. We used to have a decent and respectful working arrangement. But if he reverts to his sexual game playing or if he does anything to get back at me for speaking up, I reserve my right to bring this to another meeting and at that time I'll probably ask that one of us needs to be transferred.

Margo's boss, who was sufficiently nervous about his job and his marriage, did manage to control his sexual comments from that day forward. However, Margo's action steps and the change in her boss's behavior did not fully resolve the situation.

As you sometimes find in companies where there is a lot of gossip and innuendo, some rumors began to emerge that once again created a hostile and uncomfortable working environment for Margo. This brings us to the third difficulty that many people face when they speak up against sexual harassment or discrimination in the workplace.

Psychological Factor #3: No One Likes to Have Their Sexuality or Their Private Life Scrutinized by Colleagues at Work

The third reason why most people keep silent about harassment and gender issues at work is because we know from experience that once you open up this can of worms you often find your own sexuality and private actions being talked about by people at work who have no right to judge your personal life.

For example, in the Clarence Thomas hearings, one of the reactions that took place repeatedly after Anita Hill came forward with her descriptions of sexual harassment is that several individuals began to attack her credibility and character.

Senator Alan Simpson of Wyoming dramatically told the nation on television that there were many accusations coming into his office about Anita Hill's own misbehaviors.

This later turned out to be a false statement, yet it began to look as though Professor Hill rather than Judge Thomas was being evaluated.

Then Senator Arlen Specter of Pennsylvania tried repeatedly to accuse Anita Hill of perjury. One witness accused Anita Hill of being a ''scorned woman'' with a propensity to imagine fantasies that weren't true. Other people called Anita Hill a prude. Still others spread rumors that she might be a lesbian. A painful atmosphere of rumors and innuendo erupted over whether Professor Hill or Judge Thomas was telling the truth.

Despite all the name-calling and false rumors thrown at her, Anita Hill continued to speak up against harassment in a caring and articulate fashion. Not only did she gain the respect of millions of men and women nationwide who admired her courage, but she also retained the love and respect of most of her colleagues and students at the University of Oklahoma, as well as her family and her friends.

In Margo's case, after she and the director of human resources stood up to Margo's boss and got him to stop his harassing behavior, their challenges continued for several months. A number of rumors and innuendoes began to disrupt Margo's work life once again. One rumor stated that Margo and her boss had been having an affair. Another rumor claimed that Margo was involved in a ménage à trois with her boss and his wife. Still another rumor (which sounded a lot like a rumor from the Anita Hill/Clarence Thomas situation) insisted that Margo was secretly in love with her boss and that she merely imagined his harassment.

As you often find, the rumor mill responded to a woman claiming sexual harassment by putting the accuser's reputation on trial. I wish I could tell you that this kind of thing will not happen to you in your situation at work. But the odds are strong that someone will attempt at some point to discredit you because they feel threatened by the truth you are telling.

In light of these painful realities, how do you gather up

the courage to speak out against harassment and discrimination when you know there's a strong likelihood your honesty will be responded to with rumors and comments about your own private life? Is it worth subjecting yourself to that kind of hostility in order to correct the harassment or discrimination you've been putting up with?

No one can make that decision for you, but I urge you to keep in mind that there are ways to reduce or eliminate the amount of rumor-spreading that often occurs in situations like these.

If you decide to take action to stop the harassment or discrimination at your job, I recommend you also:

- Ask several of your friends and allies to take charge of what professionals in the public relations field call "rumor control management." That means these friends and allies need to squash any rumors they hear. They need to correct any misinformation or innuendoes that are beginning to spread. They need to speak up on your behalf whenever it is appropriate so that people you work with understand your point of view and are not swayed by half-truths, lies, or rumors.

- Make sure you have a firm written agreement from any company officials that your comments to them about the harassment or discrimination incidents will be kept confidential.

- Make sure the person who is accused of harassment or discrimination knows that any retaliation measures, including the spreading of rumors or character slurs, is also a form of harassment that could have serious legal and financial consequences for the person spreading these false statements.

If you care about your own peace of mind and the way women are treated where you work, don't be intimidated by the threat of a nasty rumor. Don't let anyone scare you out of going forward with a justified claim of harassment or discrimination.

Even if you get called a bitch, a tease, a slut, a prude, a spoilsport, a man-hater, a liar, or any other words that are usually thrown about to silence victims of mistreatment, simply recognize that you are stirring up the waters in a positive way. You can expect some turbulence, but with the support of your friends and the rightness of your claims, you will make an impact that will eventually improve some of the problems where you work.

In Margo's case, she took this advice and asked her friends and allies to help her with rumor control management. For the next several months, Margo was somewhat discouraged each time she heard another false rumor that was being spread, but she also was heartened to find out that with each rumor there was a strong and concerted effort by her friends and allies to correct the misinformation.

Margo became a lot stronger as a human being as a result of standing up for herself at work. Her boss and the rumor-spreaders at work eventually learned that she wasn't going to crumble and that they had underestimated her strength and her resourcefulness.

As Margo looked back a year later at the entire sexual harassment situation she had faced, she commented, "I still feel badly that this had to happen at all. But I feel good at how I handled it and how I let people know that I'm not a victim any longer."

What Will You Say the Next Time a Testosteroni Challenges You?

So far, we've covered several ways of protecting yourself and being successful in response to incidents of sexual harassment and discrimination. But there's one more key issue that's necessary in order to deal with most Testosteronis— namely, how to respond effectively and not get flustered right at the moment when the Testosteroni says or does something inappropriate at work.

If a Testosteroni makes a sexual advance toward you, how do you keep your cool and respond in a professional fashion? If an intimidating male at work comes out with a demeaning or sexist remark that makes you feel uncomfortable, how do you make sure not to underreact or not to overreact? If someone at work is insulting or discriminatory against you, how do you stand up for yourself without alienating people you have to work with or without encouraging someone to keep treating you badly?

In other words, what exactly are you going to say the next time a Testosteroni challenges you at work?

The Two Best Comeback Lines

If you happen to get into a close encounter with a hostile or horny person at work who is making it difficult for you to do your job, here are the two best responses that I've found work wonders in many situations. See which of the following feel the most useful to you and your challenges at work.

Comeback Line #1: "Hold on for a Minute. Let's Talk About This as Two Professional Colleagues."

If you practice this line ahead of time with a friend or counselor, it will be extremely handy during a difficult encounter with a Testosteroni. If someone tries to pressure you sexually, you can take charge and cool off this person's ardor without sounding prudish or bitchy. Simply take a deep breath in and out as you summon up your strength and say, "Hold on for a minute. Let's talk about this as two professional colleagues."

Immediately you have changed the context from one of sexuality and pressure to one of professionalism and rationality. The other person will be surprised at how composed and together you seem to be. The other person might also be startled into facing the reality that you are not looking at the situation as a sexual one whatsoever, but rather as a professional work situation in which sexual advances are inappropriate.

Or if someone makes a hostile or discriminatory remark about women that makes you feel unwelcome or uncomfortable, you don't need to get huffy or preachy. Simply by saying, "Hold on for a minute. Let's talk about this as two professional colleagues," you reestablish the teamwork and camaraderie that you will need in order to get this person to treat you as an equal.

For example, Louise is a middle manager in a predominantly male company. For years she has put up with sexist jokes, hostile remarks, and persistent digs from other managers.

Recently, however, she lost her closest friend to breast cancer and her younger sister got divorced from a man who was violent and verbally abusive. In addition, Louise has been working long hours each day and sometimes coming to work on weekends because her company has been going through a difficult economic time.

Louise explains,

> I used to be able to ignore some of the crap my male colleagues would say to me. They were just testing me to see if I was willing to play by their rules. But lately I'm simply not in the mood anymore to hear sexist jokes or demeaning comments about breasts where I work, especially after my friend's illness and my sister's situation with her abusive husband. I still have a great sense of humor and I still enjoy a good laugh with these guys. But in order to do my job these days I don't want to hear my colleagues telling me some demeaning or hostile jokes that are meant to put women down.

A few weeks ago, Louise worked overtime for seven straight days to put together a major presentation to some important customers. She was optimistic about this crucial meeting, but as soon as the meeting began, her boss started his opening speech by telling two "big knockers" jokes that were put-downs of women. Louise decided to say something to him about it, because as she recalls the incident,

> My boss knew I'd worked extra hard to make this meeting a success. And then, right in front of me, he's telling these anti-women jokes. Really in bad taste. I felt like rushing out of there and never coming back. But I'm not willing to let his continual put-downs of women cost me my job.

Instead of overreacting or verbally attacking her boss, Louise used the comeback line we had practiced earlier. She took her boss aside after the presentation meeting and she said, "I need to talk to you about those two jokes in your speech."

Her boss immediately got defensive and patronizing. He said, "Oh now don't get all worked up about this, Louise. You're not one of those feminists, are you?"

Louise took a deep breath in and out. Then she summoned up her most take-charge voice as she said calmly, "Hold on for a minute. Let's talk about this as two professional colleagues."

For the next five minutes, Louise and her boss had a reasonable, professional conversation in which she told him that it seemed out of line for him to be telling anti-women jokes during an important presentation, especially since the majority of the hard work on the project had been done by Louise, who is a woman.

Louise recalls the conversation:

> It was interesting to be using my most professional and take-charge voice in this exchange with my boss. In the past, I would have kept silent and let my resentments eat away at my insides. Or I might have blown up and called him all sorts of names like, "You are such an insensitive sexist pig." But that always gets him to be more insulting and more patronizing to me. So this time I got to see what it's like to point something out

to him as though we are two professional colleagues, equals of a sort. He was a lot less defensive and I think he actually could see that I was right. He had been out of line with those jokes and he had treated me pretty badly.

I can't say he's changed completely since that conversation, but he is a little more respectful and considerate now that he knows I'm going to bring these things up to him every time he crosses the line.

Like Louise, most women feel trapped and powerless to respond to the sexual and discriminatory remarks they are confronted with at work. You feel like it's a no-win situation. Either you keep silent and essentially encourage the Testosteronis to keep insulting you, or you blurt out an angry response that has them laughing at you and accusing you of being too sensitive.

But if you think of yourself as an adult professional who deserves to be treated with respect, you can look the Testosteroni straight in the eye and say, "Hold on for a minute. Let's talk about this as two professional colleagues." That sets the tone for a conversation in which you and the other person are not just man and woman, but more importantly, you are a competent professional who deserves to be treated much better than this person has been treating you.

Comeback Line #2: "Stop! What You Just Said is Not Good for My Career, and It Could Be Dangerous for Your Career."

This second response is a little stronger, almost like an abrupt wake-up call that says, "Hey buddy, I am not going to let you force me into a hostile environment and I'm prepared to make your career very uncomfortable if you don't cut it out right now."

But you will notice that it still has a calm and professional tone to it. You don't seem to be overreacting when you say, "Stop! What you just said is not good for my career, and it could be dangerous for your career.'' You simply are stating a fact and warning this person that he still has a chance to avoid trouble if he cuts the nonsense immediately.

A good example of how effective this comeback line can be is Gina's situation with her most important client, Raymond. Gina is an account executive for an advertising agency and she has the responsibility for keeping her client happy so that his firm will stay with Gina's agency. Unfortunately, Raymond is a very macho and self-centered marketing executive who has been trying for the past six months to get Gina to sleep with him.

As Gina told me during a counseling session,

Raymond just won't take no for an answer. In fact, the more I get flustered and uncomfortable from his constant sexual remarks to me, the more he seems to get aroused and determined to break down my resistance. I don't want to lose this important account, and I resent the fact that he's got me worried and nervous all the time that I'm going to say the wrong thing and he might get retaliatory against me or take his business elsewhere.

After practicing the second comeback line, ''Stop! What you just said is not good for my career, and it could be dangerous for your career,'' Gina realized that she didn't have to remain in a powerless position with Raymond. She could let him know clearly that his continued harassment of her was possibly going to force her to speak up to his bosses, to an attorney, or to their colleagues in the small circle of marketing executives and account executives who know one another fairly well. But she could say it with a calm professionalism that would convince him she was serious and strong enough to follow through on her threat.

A few weeks later, Gina was at a lunch meeting with Raymond when he told her he had arranged for a hotel room and that he wanted her to spend the afternoon with him there. Gina quickly paid for Raymond's lunch check as she told him calmly and professionally, "Stop! What you just said is not good for my career, and it could be dangerous for your career."

Raymond asked what she meant by that, and Gina explained that she had been documenting his inappropriate behavior for several months and was prepared to go public with the documentation if he didn't cut it out. With a gentle and relaxed tone of voice, Gina also explained that she was willing to continue working with him and would not expose him to his bosses and to the industry if he was willing to stop pressuring her for sex.

Raymond was surprised. He had never met a woman who not only could say no to his sexual advances but also could turn the tables and put him at risk of losing his job and jeopardizing his career. At first, Raymond was angry as he said, "You bitch. You'd never do a thing like that, would you?"

Gina remained calm and in control as she explained to Raymond, "I definitely could do that, but I'm letting you know now that if you stop the remarks and stick to business, I'll keep all my documentation to myself. But I have to warn you that if you do anything against me or my agency, I'll have to bring out the documentation and explain to everyone why you're acting this way."

For the next several days, Gina was worried about how Raymond might respond. She documented what had been discussed at the lunch meeting and she wrote a confidential letter to her employee relations manager that she needed his support if Raymond took any action against her or the agency.

A week later, the phone rang, and Raymond asked her to lunch to discuss one of the print media campaigns they had been preparing together. At that lunch meeting, Raymond was professional and businesslike. He didn't bring up anything sexual and neither did Gina. For the next several months Raymond continued to treat Gina with professional respect. Then Gina found out that Raymond would soon be leaving his job to join another company in a different part of the state.

While not every Testosteroni gets the message as quickly and as clearly as Raymond did, you will find that if you take charge and change the situation from a sexual one to a career/legal one, most Testosteronis will back off. Most men will not consciously jeopardize their jobs or their careers by pursuing a woman who they know will turn them in for their inappropriate and illegal activities.

I urge you to keep finding ways to get the external support and the internal strength you will need to stand up to anyone at work who is harassing you or discriminating against you because you are a woman. Remember that no one deserves to work under conditions like that. Perhaps one day women will be treated as respected equals wherever they work. Until that day, make sure you know how to protect yourself if you encounter a Testosteroni.

10

A Few More Ideas for Taking Charge of Your Situation

In the previous nine chapters, I have attempted to give you some creative options for responding more effectively to certain people at work who tend to treat you badly.

In this final chapter, I want to look at some additional possibilities that might bring you more satisfaction and success at work.

When someone at your job treats you badly, these incidents can become a spark that opens up new insights and new opportunities for you. Take a few moments to consider the following examples of people whose work lives were transformed by how they responded to an incident in which someone at work treated them badly. Notice if any of these examples give you some ideas of things you might want to pursue:

The Man with the Neon Sign on His Forehead

A few years ago, an intelligent and creative design engineer named Jerome came to one of my workshops and told me about his problems dealing with an extremely difficult boss.

At first, when I listened to Jerome's troubles with his boss, I was caught up in the details of how obnoxious and unfair Jerome's current supervisor tended to be.

But then, after a few therapy sessions with Jerome, I realized that Jerome had been treated unfairly not only by his current boss but by several previous bosses. At each of Jerome's previous jobs, things had gone well for a few months and then there would be a gradual falling out between Jerome and his supervisors.

Jerome told me he couldn't understand why with each boss there was an inevitable souring of the work relationship.

> I don't get it. I work hard, I try not to make waves, and I get along with most of my colleagues. But at each of my jobs, I eventually find myself working for someone who singles me out for verbal abuse and excessive criticism, or who treats me unfairly. It's happened four times in a row and I wish I could figure out what's the reason. Is there something I'm doing that causes my supervisors to see me as a problem? If I knew what it is I tend to do that pisses them off, then I'd work to change whatever is causing the problem. What could it be?

Jerome was asking an excellent question. If someone is having a problem at work and that problem keeps showing up with each subsequent job, there might be something he or she is doing that's asking for trouble or creating tensions at work.

Now I'm not saying that in all cases if someone mistreats you at work it's definitely your fault. Sometimes you can be an innocent bystander who got picked out, and you didn't ask for it whatsoever. In many cases, people at work treat us badly not because of anything we did to provoke them but because they were already upset and were looking for someone to victimize.

But with some individuals who get mistreated at job after job, there is something they are doing that antagonizes or provokes the people they work with. In the majority of cases, I've found the problem tends to be one of the following habits.

Provocation #1: Lateness

If you tend to be late or sometimes unreliable at work, it will at some point provoke a negative response from most bosses or customers who are relying on you. I urge anyone who has a habit of chronic lateness to come to terms with that problem in therapy so that they don't keep provoking people at work to resent or mistreat them. By finding out the reasons why you have acquired the unfortunate habit of lateness, you can begin step by step to get better at being on time and preventing the mistreatment that you've been receiving from people at work who resent your lateness.

Provocation #2: An Attitude of "I Don't Want to Be Here"

If you are sluggishly going through the motions at work and you don't want to be there, sooner or later your ambivalence about your job is going to affect the people you work with and cause them to resent your negativity. I recommend that while you still have a job, now is the time to work with a therapist or a career counselor to find out what you *do* want to do and what fears and obstacles you'll need to overcome in order to turn your ideas into reality. I have seen numerous examples of people who were treated badly at work because of their "I don't want to be here" attitude, but when they did discover and pursue their heartfelt work dreams their attitude improved dramatically and people were excited to be working with them.

Provocation #3: A Rebelliousness Against Authority Figures

In many cases in which someone gets mistreated at each subsequent job, it turns out that this individual tends to be rebellious or antagonistic around authority figures in general. Unless a person comes to terms with this rebellious tendency that usually goes back to his or her childhood, it will continue to provoke tension with the inevitable authority figures that show up in almost every work environment.

In Jerome's therapy sessions, we explored these three possibilities, but none of them seemed to be the issue that was causing each of Jerome's bosses to treat him badly.

Lateness was not the issue because Jerome was rarely late for work and tended to complete his assignments without procrastinating very much. The attitude of "I don't want to be here" was not the problem because Jerome was hard-working and usually very interested in the projects he did at work. Nor was rebelliousness against authority the issue for Jerome. On the contrary, Jerome tended to be slightly deferential and overly polite to his bosses and superiors at work. Growing up in the South, Jerome had learned to appear humble and to avoid any appearance of disrespect for elders or authority figures. Jerome was more likely to be overly compliant toward authority figures and not very defiant or rebellious.

A Fourth Reason Why You Might Get Treated Badly at Work

For several weeks I couldn't seem to understand why someone as intelligent and competent as Jerome was getting victimized by one supervisor after another.

Then a possible clue emerged during one of our counseling sessions. I had noticed on several occasions that Jerome had a habit of getting nervous and apologizing when he was about to say something strong or heartfelt.

For instance, on one occasion he was describing a fascinating project he had designed at work and he prefaced his remarks by saying, "This might sound stupid, but—"

On another occasion he was talking about his extensive training in design engineering and he prefaced his remarks by saying, "This might not make any sense, but—"

I asked him if he was aware that he sometimes seemed to be apologizing for his words and undermining his own statements by saying things like, "This might sound stupid," or "This might not make any sense."

Jerome smiled shyly and said, "Yeah, I do that a lot."

"Do you do it at work?" I asked.

"I think I do."

"Do your bosses react in any way when you say things like, 'This might sound stupid' or 'This might not make any sense?'"

Jerome thought for a moment, and then he said, "Yeah, I've noticed that they seem to be impatient and a little irritated with me when I downplay my statements like that. And they assume that I'm a pushover that they can walk all over."

Does Jerome's habit of apologizing or downplaying his statements at work sound like you or anyone you know?

I have found that even some of the most competent and intelligent men and women tend to have this self-defeating habit. For instance, in the past few weeks, when you have been at work with an Angry Screamer, a Saccharine Snake, a Space Case, an Invalidator, a Cold Shoulder, or a Testosteroni, have you:

- Felt intimidated or tongue-tied?
- Apologized ahead of time for anything you thought this person might not like?
- Downplayed any of your own accomplishments or opinions?
- Worried about whether this person was going to criticize you or oppose you?
- Tried so hard to win this person's approval that you began to feel clumsy, awkward, or self-defeating?

If you answered yes to any of the above questions, then you might be one of the many individuals who, like Jerome, feels and acts unsure of yourself around certain important people at work.

What Can Be Done About It?

The first step in making sure you don't keep downplaying your self-worth in workplace settings is to find out what in your past experiences has made you this cautious and apologetic. Certainly there is a good reason why you've learned to second-guess yourself like this. But now this second-guessing and apologizing may be causing other people at work to become impatient or irritated with you.

For the next few weeks, Jerome and I began to explore why he had acquired this self-deprecating habit of apologizing for his statements and undermining his own assertions.

We discovered that when Jerome was growing up with an extremely domineering and demanding father, he often felt intimidated by his father's skeptical and harsh comments. Jerome recalled, "Growing up with my father, there was no way to feel acknowledged or appreciated. He put down everything I did and said. He made fun of my creative talents and he kept telling me I'd never amount to anything."

Even after Jerome had done well in college and had studied for a master's degree in design engineering, his father was still skeptical and demeaning. According to Jerome, "At my graduation he told me that all of my professors were idiots and that I should have gone into medicine like my older brother. I remember trying to say something to defend myself, but by father could always silence me with that angry glare of his. I knew not to get him mad at me again."

So as a result of his intimidating upbringing with his domineering father, Jerome had acquired the habit of being hesitant and apologetic whenever he spoke up to an authority figure. That tendency, coupled with his Southern traditional background, made him extremely cautious and compliant around authority figures.

The Neon Sign

I call Jerome's case "The Man with the Neon Sign on His Forehead" because in essence Jerome had made a decision on how to protect himself against authority figures like his father. Like many insecure or cautious individuals who grew up with an intimidating parent, Jerome had put up the equivalent of a neon sign on his forehead that said, "Don't yell at me. Don't get mad at me. I'll apologize for what I have to say even before I say it. Just don't get upset with me."

I have found that many people have the equivalent of a flashing neon sign at work that says how they want to be treated. For example, you might have an expression on your face and a way of speaking in business meetings that says, "I'm confident. I've done a lot of preparation and I know this is important."

Or you might be like Jerome and have an expression on your face and a way of speaking that says, "I'm scared. I think you're not going to like what I have to say. I'm willing to apologize ahead of time for whatever I say in case you don't like it."

When you say or do self-deprecating things like that in a workplace setting, it often becomes a self-fulfilling prophesy. You expect to be treated with disapproval or tension. You flash a neon message on your face or in your apologetic statements such as, "This might sound stupid, but—" or "This might not make any sense, but—" Then, as Jerome found with each of his supervisors, the response you get is impatience, irritation, and disapproval. Even if you are well-prepared and competent, you elicit a negative reaction from the other person by your cautious or self-deprecating way of presenting yourself.

Breaking the Habit

As with any self-defeating behavior, breaking the habit of apologizing for yourself might not be easy. You may need to come to terms with a lifetime of insecure feelings and worries in order to start sounding and acting more confident in workplace interactions.

Fortunately for Jerome, he was willing to work hard in therapy to uncover and resolve many of his insecure feelings and self-defeating habits from his painful upbringing. But in order to start sounding and acting more confident in business settings, Jerome also needed an extra boost that came from a simple exercise he began practicing on a regular basis.

To boost Jerome's self-esteem and to break his habit of second-guessing himself in front of important individuals at work, I suggested he utilize a simple device that has been successful for many people and that I call "The Self-Respect Notecard." It works like this:

The Self-Respect Notecard
On a 3"×5" card write the following words.

The more I respect my own hard work and persistence,
the more I will bring about respect from other people.

Keep the card in your wallet or purse and look at it once a day (or more often in stressful situations). When you look at this notecard and say these words to yourself several times at the beginning of a stressful workday or just prior to an important phone call or meeting, you may find some excellent results.

I have suggested this device to many women and men who had the habit of underestimating their worth or second-guessing themselves around intimidating people. In nearly every case, there was an improvement caused in part by practicing with this notecard at least once a day and gradually believing and internalizing the statement, ''The more I respect my own hard work and persistence, the more I will bring about respect from other people.''

I remember one woman named Annette who used this Self-Respect Notecard to help her overcome her chronic habit of criticizing and not finishing her own creative projects. Prior to using this exercise, Annette had been so self-critical and perfectionistic about her creative work that she was unable to finish most of her projects and she dreaded letting anyone see them.

After several months of counseling and her daily regimen of repeating this affirmation statement to herself, Annette began to change somewhat. She explained,

> I stopped being so bloody critical and so worried about everything I do. Instead of trying to be perfect and not wanting to let anyone see my work, I slowly realized that my goal could be to enjoy and respect my own hard work and my persistence—to just appreciate what I'm doing instead of judging it or worry about how others will judge it. That freed me up a bit to start finishing some of my incomplete projects and to let people see what I've done.

Something remarkable happens to your attitude about your own work and the way you present yourself to important people when you have been repeating to yourself each day the words, ''The more I respect my own hard work and persistence, the more I will bring about respect from other people.'' It, too, can become a self-fulfilling prophesy because of how it boosts your self-esteem and allows you to project more confidence to those who previously intimidated you at work.

When you give yourself a daily affirmation of self-respect, your insecurities gradually begin to lessen. It becomes less likely that you will undermine yourself at work with remarks that sound self-deprecating or apologetic. Your initial change of attitude also leads in most cases to an external change in the way you present yourself. Your stronger and more confident presentation of yourself at work encourages others to start treating you with more respect.

But sometimes it takes a while for results to show up and for a lifelong habit of second-guessing yourself to disappear. In Jerome's case, his therapy sessions and his use of this Self- Respect Notecard didn't result in any miraculous overnight changes. It took Jerome several months before he completely stopped his habit of apologizing and second-guessing himself in stressful work situations. It took a few additional months before his boss fully realized the change in Jerome and stopped reacting to Jerome with impatience and irritation. But finally the notecard and the therapy work paid off. According to Jerome,

> Something changed inside of me from coming to terms with my intimidating father and from reminding myself each day that I need to respect my own hard work and persistence. That change within me began to affect the way I presented myself at work. Slowly I became a lot more professional-sounding and a lot less insecure in how I spoke to my boss and other intimidating people.
>
> It took a while for my boss to see that I've changed, but he gradually stopped being as crabby and impatient around me. He now talks to me with a somewhat different attitude, as if he's no longer picking on me for my being insecure or vulnerable. Instead, he seems to trust me a little bit more and he knows I'm reliable and professional.
>
> I still see him get crabby and impatient with other colleagues at work, especially those who seem apologetic or insecure around him. My boss will always be someone who instinctively picks on anyone who appears weak or vulnerable. But since he no longer sees me that way, he treats me like a respected professional.

And I have no intention of going backward to the old days when he treated me with impatience and contempt.

The Importance of Being More Professional

You will notice that in addition to Jerome's feeling more self-confident and acting less apologetic, he also mentions his becoming more professional in his style of work.

Throughout this book, I have emphasized repeatedly that if you want to be treated better at work, you first need to find out what specific things you can improve in order to be perceived as a valuable professional and not as a potential victim.

Just as Jerome and many others have found, when you are dealing with an intimidating person at work, you can't change the fact that this person seems to want to victimize anyone who is weak or vulnerable. But you can gradually change the way he or she perceives you, so that you will eventually be seen as a respected professional colleague and not as an easy target for mistreatment.

In your own work situation, what specific things could you begin doing to increase the likelihood that you will be perceived as a professional and not as a victim?

- Is there anything you want to change about your clothing, appearance, or way of presenting yourself at work to make sure you are taken seriously and not treated as a nobody or a potential victim?
- Is there anything you want to change about the way you express opinions and present your ideas at work so that you can avoid the mistreatment that comes to those who are apologetic or self-deprecating?
- Is there anything you can do to improve your access to information and influence where you work so that you

won't be left out of important discussions or any meetings where crucial decisions are made?

• Is there anything you can do to feel and act in a more professional fashion so that others see you as a reliable, confident human being rather than a potential victim?

I urge you to start today and keep moving toward whatever positive steps you feel can help you improve your professional image at work. Because, as the notecard says, the more you respect your own hard work and persistence, the more you will bring about respect from other people.

The Woman Who Stopped Feeling Like a Victim

In some situations, you can try many things to improve your work relationship with a difficult individual, but you don't seem to make any progress. As the months and the years pass by, you become increasingly discouraged. You wonder if you'll ever feel good again about your work life.

But as I've stated repeatedly in this book, there are ways to improve your situation even if the other person doesn't change. Natalie's case is a good example that can give you a few more useful ideas of what to do even if your adversary at work has no intention to budge an inch.

I call Natalie's case "The Woman Who Stopped Feeling Like a Victim." If you had met her fourteen months ago, you would be amazed at how different she looks and acts today as compared to when she first sought help for her difficulties at work.

When I first spoke to her at a workshop, Natalie had a challenging and exciting job working for a medium-size consulting firm. She had taken that job seven years earlier because she enjoyed the intellectual aspect of her assignments and she liked working with a variety of interesting clients.

But her problem from the start had been that one of the senior partners, whose name is Frederick, is a terror to be around. Natalie described this senior partner of her consulting firm.

Frederick is extremely brilliant, but he uses his intelligence like a weapon. He loves to provoke a disagreement and then beat you down with his intellect. At nearly every department meeting he finds someone to pick a fight with, and by the end of the meeting at least one person ends up feeling crushed or humiliated.

When Natalie came for counseling fourteen months ago, she was concerned that working for Frederick was beginning to be hazardous to her health. She had frequent headaches, skin flare-ups, and digestive problems that no medical doctor could seem to resolve. She seemed depressed and she reported feeling moody and short-tempered with her two teenage children. Natalie told me,

It worries me how much I'm taking the frustrations from work home with me. My friends tell me to just leave the tensions at the office, but that doesn't seem to be possible for me. I'm the kind of person who feels great when my life is going great and who really feels anxious when things are going badly. So with all the tension at work day after day, it's as though I'm anxious or depressed much of the time.

When we began to explore her situation, Natalie toyed with the idea of possibly starting her own consulting business and getting away from Frederick's toxic energy. But she decided against it for several reasons. First, she felt she needed to hold onto her current medical and dental plans or else she might lose a lot of money because of her own medical bills and some huge dental bills incurred by her two children. Second, she was only a few years away from qualifying for an excellent pension program at her current firm. Third, she had been participating in a profit-sharing program that would be dramatically reduced if she decided to leave her company and go elsewhere. Fourth, she felt close to several other people at her firm, each of whom shared her disgust with Frederick's oppressive style.

In addition to these reasons for not starting her own company, Natalie also told me,

> Until the economic climate gets significantly stronger, I'm not willing to take a risk like that. I think it would be a mistake to start my own consulting firm at a time when most of my potential clients are cutting back on their expenditures.

So the challenge for Natalie, as for many others who are forced to work in close proximity with an extremely unpleasant individual, was twofold:

- How to take better care of herself physically and emotionally whenever she had to have a close encounter of the Frederick kind
- How to stop feeling victimized and start enjoying her job again, even if Frederick refused to change very much

The Road That Leads from Victimization to Empowerment

As in many cases that I've seen over the years, Natalie didn't change overnight because of one specific exercise or technique. It took her several months using several creative steps before she began to feel a lot healthier and less victimized by her situation at work. Here's what worked for Natalie and what might be some creative options for your own situation.

Step 1: Protecting Herself Against Frederick's Toxic Energy: Natalie began to practice the exercises listed in Chapter 4 on how to deal with an Angry Screamer and in

Chapter 7 on how to respond to an Invalidator. The one she liked the best was the exercise in Chapter 4 in which she protected herself against Frederick's domineering style by saying to herself, "Hear the valuable stuff. Ignore the anger. It's not yours."

Natalie explains,

> I used to sit there, totally vulnerable and unprotected at a meeting where Frederick was ripping me or someone else to shreds. Now I say to myself whenever I hear him shouting or attacking someone verbally, "Hear the valuable stuff. Ignore the anger. It's not yours."
>
> Knowing that I can protect myself against his angry tone of voice helps a lot. I can sift through what he's saying and find out if there's something valuable there that will help me do my job better. But I make sure to block out his hostile, demeaning way of talking. For the first time in years, I'm protected, so I don't wind up carrying his anger around with me the rest of the day.

I recommend that if you feel victimized by someone at work, you need to go back to the earlier chapters and find the exercises that give you the most protection and inner strength. As Natalie discovered, you can learn to sit in a meeting with an abusive person and protect yourself emotionally while still hearing whatever valuable information is available. Using one or more of the exercises described throughout this book, you can find a way to protect yourself and not get victimized by someone who is extremely unpleasant to be around.

Step 2: Taking Charge of Your Daily Schedule to Make Sure You Include Those Activities You Do Enjoy: The next step for Natalie was to stop spending her entire day thinking about how unpleasant it is to work with someone like Frederick. Instead, she began to start scheduling in more time for those aspects of her job that she used to find enjoyable.

Too often we tend to focus only on what's going wrong at work. We become obsessed with the difficult person who is getting on our nerves. Or we spend a lot of time and energy mulling over our interactions with someone who is abusive or unpleasant.

I'm not suggesting that you deny or ignore the problem you are having with a difficult person at work, but I am saying that you have the right to escape from those tensions every so often. In order to take charge of your work life and stop feeling so victimized, you may need to make a list of exactly what activities you used to enjoy and would look forward to experiencing more often. For example, when I asked Natalie to make a list of five things she used to enjoy about her job, she wrote:

- I loved going out to lunch with someone I care about.
- I enjoyed solving problems for one of my clients whose situation was very close to my heart.
- I loved that feeling of teamwork that happens some-times when several people are working hard together on an important deadline.
- I loved the creative moments when I'd go for a walk or I'd take a few minutes alone in my office to brainstorm about something that needed a creative solution.
- I enjoyed going to industry seminars and association events to learn new information, keep up on important trends, and stay in touch with certain people in my industry.

Unfortunately, because of the tensions Natalie had been experiencing with Frederick, she had stopped making time for most of these enjoyable activities. It had been several weeks since she had gone to lunch with anyone she cared about. It had been several months since she felt a sense of teamwork and excitement with any of her colleagues. It had been far too long since she took time for a walk or some quiet moments to brainstorm creatively. It had been almost a year since she'd attended any industry seminars or association events.

Like many people who feel victimized by someone at work, Natalie had forgotten to schedule very much time for the things that used to make her job exciting and satisfying.

Does her situation sound at all like your own? Are you possibly spending too much time and energy dwelling on the person at work whom you can't stand? Are you neglecting to schedule for each day some activities that you enjoy and that you look forward to experiencing?

When you think about your own daily schedule, consider the following:

- What specific things can you do starting today to reduce the amount of time you spend in close proximity to the person at work you can't stand?
- What specific things can you do starting today to spend less time worrying about this individual?
- What specific things can you do starting today to make each work week more satisfying, with time set aside for the activities and people you enjoy?

After Natalie and I discussed her list of five enjoyable activities, she began to schedule more time to pursue these and other fulfilling aspects of her job. She began going out to lunch with a good friend or a fun colleague at least once a week. She began setting up more opportunities for brainstorming and creative interactions with people she enjoyed at work. She began attending more industry seminars and association events, where she got acknowledged by her peers for her involvement in some worthwhile activities. She also spent at least one day a month researching and testing out some of her ideas for possibly starting a business of her own when the timing was right.

As a result of these scheduling changes, Natalie was successfully taking charge of making sure there was something on her list of things to do each day that she could look forward to enjoying.

Natalie told me after a few months of this new approach to her work schedule,

> I no longer spend my time feeling like I'm a victim or that I'm trapped forever working for Frederick. I've reestablished some good contacts with people at some other companies who will let me know if there are any job opportunities opening up where they work. I've also started meeting one day a month with a woman from another firm who might eventually become my business partner if the timing is right and if she and I decide to follow through on some of our ideas for starting a business. So I don't feel stuck or victimized as though my situation with Frederick is the only option I'll ever have. And since I've begun putting at least one enjoyable activity on my list of things to do each day, I feel like I've taken back control of my work life. There's a lot more to this job than just having to deal with Frederick. And some of those activities are things I find exciting and pleasurable.

I recommend that on your own list of activities for each day, you make sure you have included some of the things you used to enjoy about your job. Be sure to include some diversions and escapes that can make each workday a lot more fun and interesting.

Even though you work with someone unpleasant, you still have the right to take charge of your own schedule and your own peace of mind. As Natalie found, the more you schedule those activities that feel enjoyable to you, the less you will feel trapped or controlled by the difficult person with whom you are forced to work.

Step 3: The Next Time You Are with This Difficult Person, Imagine That You Are His or Her Parent (and That This Person is Your Emotionally Troubled Child): The final step for Natalie was to change the way she felt and talked when she was confronted by Frederick face to face.

Too often we feel childlike and powerless around certain intimidating people at work. Yet if you look at the situation in a different light, you might see that you are far more adult and mature than the person screaming at you in front of everyone at work. This person's nasty comments and temper tantrums reveal the fact that he or she is emotionally troubled, like an anxious child who needs a strong, reassuring parent.

When you are confronted by an angry or intimidating boss or customer, it helps tremendously to imagine that you are this person's parent. But rather than being a mean or judgmental parent, imagine yourself to be a calming and reassuring parental influence when this person gets angry or upset.

Instead of being intimidated by this person's harsh words, summon up your inner strength and calm this person with the soothing voice of a parent who is firmly in control. If this volatile boss or customer begins to criticize you or attack you with a verbal assault, simply say, "It's all right. Don't worry. Let's talk it over and we'll figure this out."

Those soothing words communicate two important things: first, that you are calm and professional; second, that you are ready and able to listen to possible ways to solve the problem that is upsetting this other person.

Even if you tend to be an anxious or cautious person at times, I'm willing to bet that there are other times when your tone of voice and your attitude are strong, confident, and self-assured. For just a moment, think about when it is that you seem to have the most confident and comforting tone of voice.

- Do you have a take-charge, confident tone with your children?
- Do you have a reassuring, soothing tone of voice with your spouse or lover, or with one of your friends or siblings?
- Is there someone at work with whom you tend to have a strong, confident, soothing tone of voice?

The trick is to take that strong and reassuring tone of voice that feels comfortable in certain life situations and bring it into your challenging interactions with the person at work who you find most intimidating or difficult. If you can act and sound as soothing and reassuring with this difficult person as you have done with certain other people in your life, you will be far less likely to be victimized by this individual. He or she will hear your strong and comforting tone of voice. This person will realize that you are not a pushover or a victim. While it may take time for a change to occur, there is a good likelihood that eventually you will be treated with more respect because of this change in your demeanor.

When I asked Natalie to imagine during a therapy session that she was speaking up to Frederick in a soothing but strong voice that said, "It's all right. Don't worry. Let's talk it over and we'll figure it out," it reminded her of her confrontations with her teenage son Corey.

Natalie explained to me,

I would never admit this to my boss, but my teenage son is a lot like Frederick in certain ways. They both insist on being right all the time and are very defensive if you try to argue with them. They both throw temper tantrums when they don't get their way. They both come at you with a verbal assault and all their guns blazing.

But for some reason, I'm not intimidated by my son Corey and I've always been able to be strong and firm with him. Even if he's yelling or getting upset, I have this reassuring tone in my voice and this sense that I'm still in control. After all, I am the adult, I am the parent.

Then why is it with Frederick I'm so intimidated? He's nothing but a bigger version of my insecure son Corey. I wish I could be as calm and strong and in control with Frederick as I am with my son.

So Natalie and I practiced for several weeks how to say to Frederick, "It's all right. Don't worry. Let's talk it over and we'll figure it out.'' Then an opportunity arose during an emotionally charged business meeting where Natalie was explaining how she was dealing with an important client and Frederick started shouting that she was doing it all wrong.

Instead of getting quiet or intimidated as she usually would have done, Natalie summoned up her inner strength and said to Frederick in a strong but reassuring tone of voice, "It's all right. Don't worry. Let's talk it over and we'll figure it out."

To Natalie's surprise, Frederick calmed down slightly. His tone of voice was still a little bit arrogant and defensive, but for the first time in months, Natalie didn't feel intimidated and she noticed he had softened just a little bit in response to her reassuring, take-charge approach. For the next few minutes, Natalie and Frederick were able to discuss the situation regarding this important client in an intelligent and calm fashion.

The next day when Natalie came to her therapy session, she was ecstatic. She told me, "This was such an important step for me. Not only did I not feel intimidated, but I seemed to be able to take charge and direct the conversation. I wasn't sitting there all anxious and victimized as I usually would be."

I must warn you that not every situation improves as quickly as Natalie's did. Quite often you may need to repeat these comforting words several times before the person hears how confident and in control you are. You may need to try out some variations on the theme of "It's all right. Don't worry. Let's talk it over and we'll figure it out," before you are finally viewed as a strong, supportive person to be treated with respect. But once this person sees you as a confident and reassuring force, there's a good chance the difficult individual will stop attacking you as often and will start working more cooperatively with you.

Natalie continued to be confronted occasionally by Frederick's domineering style, but she was able to remain emotionally strong and not get intimidated by him any longer. As she told me a few months later when she completed her therapy work,

> That one incident of speaking up to Frederick and calming him down wasn't the end of our struggles with each other. He still blows up at me from time to time. I still get verbally assaulted by him once in a while. But for the most part, I am no longer anxious or intimidated when I'm around him. I know how to protect myself emotionally. I know how to hear if there's any value in what he's saying without letting his hostile energy get into my system. I no longer feel like a victim or have any headaches or stomach flare-ups after my encounters with him. Most importantly, I've found a way to speak up and calm him down a bit. I'm no longer silent or defenseless when he tries to put me down or attack me verbally. And I can see he's a little more respectful of me now that I've become less of a victim and more professional-sounding around him.

A Final Thought

You may have noticed in Natalie's case, as in so many other examples in this book, that the breakthrough came not because she tried to change Frederick but because she found several ways to build up her own strength and her own professionalism. When you are dealing with someone at work who treats you badly, I hope you will remember that the goal is not to wait for the other individual to change into a completely different person. That's a very passive and unlikely approach to the situation.

If you are waiting for the other person to miraculously change before you can start enjoying your work life again, there's an old expression that says, "You should live so long!"

I urge you to keep in mind an additional piece of wisdom offered by theologian Reinhold Niebuhr that can be applied to any difficult situation at work. Niebuhr encouraged good people like yourself to say silently when confronted by a stressful situation:

> God give us grace to accept with serenity the things that cannot be changed, courage to change the things that should be changed, and the wisdom to distinguish the one from the other.

If you take that wisdom into your encounters at work, you will find that you will waste a lot less time attempting to change people who aren't likely to change. You will find yourself with added courage and persistence to change the things that can and should be changed. You will find that you can focus much better on how to improve your responses to a difficult individual and not to wait for that person to change into someone they are not.

My wish for you is that by putting the exercises and techniques of this book into practice in your daily work life, you will feel and act more professional and you will be treated with far more respect and decency. I realize that there will always be some extremely unpleasant individuals in the workplace, but I expect that from this day forward you will be far more skillful at responding to them without remaining a victim.

Notes

page

31   The line about rationalizations from the film *The Big Chill* was paraphrased from the characters written by Lawrence Kasdan and Barbara Benedek, produced by Carson Productions, released by Columbia Pictures, 1983.

50   The research on how authoritarian bosses tend to cause an increase in mistakes and accidents is summarized in Robert Blake and Jane Mouton's book, *The Managerial Grid*, Houston: Gulf Publishing Company, 1964.

79   The scenes from the film *Working Girl* were written by Kevin Wade and released by 20th Century Fox, 1989.

83   One of the researchers who has found a relationship between smiling and territorial aggression is Jane Goodall, *In the Shadow of Man*, Boston: Houghton Mifflin, 1971, p. 274.

84   The reference to Woodward and Bernstein overcoming a cover-up is detailed in the book *All the President's Men* by Carl Bernstein and Bob Woodward, New York: Simon and Schuster, 1974.

185   The scene from the film *Frankie and Johnny* was written by Terrence McNally and released by Paramount, 1991.

187   The U.S. Labor Department study that described the glass ceiling in corporate promotions was reported by Susan B. Garland in *Business Week* on April 29, 1991, p. 33 and on August 19, 1991, p. 29.

188   The survey of Fortune 500 companies that revealed the absenteeism, turnover, and lost productivity costs as a result of sexual harassment was described in *Working Woman* by Ronni Sandroff, December 1988, pp. 69–73.

190   The "reasonable woman standard" for sexual harassment cases was decided upon by the Ninth Circuit Court of Appeals in the case of *Ellison* v. *Brady* (924 F. 2d 871 [9th Cir. 1991]). The case was described in the *Los Angeles Times*, January 24, 1991, Sec. A, p. 3.

191   The "hostile work environment" ruling on prominently displayed calendar pictures of women was decided upon in the Middle District of Florida case of *Robinson* v. *Jacksonville Shipyards*, (59 LW 2470 [February 12, 1991]).

198   The illustration of why it's so difficult to speak up against mistreatment by a superior was developed by psychologist Michele Paludi of Hunter College based on a technique used by psychologist Andrea Parrot of Cornell University. This was described in the December 1991 issue (pp. 29–30) of the APA [American Psychological Association] *Monitor*, in an article written by Tori DeAngelis.

201   The hostile remarks made against Anita Hill by Senator Alan Simpson were reported by Eleanor Clift and Mark Starr in "Taking the Low Road," *Newsweek*, October 28, 1991, p. 30.

202 The hostile remarks by Senator Arlen Specter were reported in the *New York Times*, October 13, 1991, Sec. I, p. 1 and the *New York Times*, October 14, 1991, Sec. A, p. 1. A critique of Senator Specter's and Senator Simpson's tactics was written in the *Los Angeles Times*, October 16, 1991, Sec. F, p. 1.

About the Author

LEONARD FELDER has a doctorate in psychology and a master's degree in business administration. After working in New York as the Director of Research for Doubleday and Company and the Manager of Strategic Planning for American Express, he moved to Los Angeles in 1978.

Since then he has worked as a therapist and consultant, as well as leading workshops and seminars nationwide. He recently received the Distinguished Merit Citation of the National Conference of Christians and Jews for his efforts to combat racism, sexism and religious prejudice.

Dr. Felder's five previous books have sold more than 800,000 copies and have been translated into nine languages. His titles are *Learning to Love Forever, Making Peace With Yourself, A Fresh Start: How to Let Go of Emotional Baggage and Enjoy Your Life Again, When a Loved One Is Ill*, and the bestseller *Making Peace With Your Parents*, which won the 1985 Book of the Year Award from *Medical Self-Care Magazine*. A frequent guest on radio and television programs, Dr. Felder has appeared on "Oprah Winfrey," "Sally Jessy Raphael," "Sonya Live on CNN," "NBC News," and many other news and interview shows.

For more information about counseling or workshops with the author, you can contact him by writing: Leonard Felder, Ph. D., 11665 West Olympic Boulevard, Suite 301, Los Angeles, CA 90064, or by calling (310) 477-1288.